RESILIENT BY DESIGN

Cybersecurity and SD-WAN Synergy for Enterprise and IoT Ecosystems

Vishwanath Hiremath
Dharnisha Narasappa

notionpress.com
INDIA · SINGAPORE · MALAYSIA

ISBN

Hardcase 979-8-90479-299-2
Paperback 979-8-90392-665-7

Contents

Chapter 1

Introduction to Cybersecurity

1.1 Introduction

Internet is among the most important inventions of modern era which have affected our life. Today internet has crossed every barrier and has changed the way we use to talk, play games, work, shop, make friends, listen music, see movies, order food, pay bill, greet your friend on his birthday/ anniversary, etc. You name it, and we have an app in place for that. It has facilitated our life by making it comfortable. Gone are the days when we have to stand in a long queue for paying our telephone and electricity bills. Now we can pay it at a click of a button from our home or office. The technology has reached to an extent that we don't even require a computer for using internet. Now we have internet enabled smartphone, palmtops, etc. through which we can remain connected to our friends, family and office 24x7. Not only internet has simplified our life but also it has brought many things within the reach of the middle class by making them cost effective. It was not long back, while making an ISD or even a STD call, the eyes were stricken on the pulse meter. The calls were very costly. ISD and STD were used to pass on urgent messages only and the rest of the routine communication was done using letters since it was a relatively very cheap. Now internet has made it possible to not only talk but use video conference using popular applications like skype, Google Meet, Zoom etc. at a very low price to a level where a one-hour video chat using internet is cheaper that the cost of sending a one-page document from Delhi to Bangalore using speed – post or courier service. Not only this, internet has changed the use of the typical devices that were used by us. Television can be used not only for watching popular tv shows and movies but can be used for calling/ video chatting with friend using internet. Mobile phone is not only used for making a call but viewing a latest movie. We can remain connected to everyone, no matter what our location is. Working parents from office can keep eye on their children at home and help them in their homework. A businessman can keep eye on his staff, office, shop, etc with a click of a button. It has facilitated our life in more than one way. Have you ever wondered from where this internet came? Let us discuss the brief history of internet and learn how this internet was invented and how it evolved to an extent that now we cannot think of our lives without it.

1.1.1 History of Internet

I don't know what the cold war between USA and Russia gave to the world, but definitely the internet is one of those very useful inventions whose foundation was laid during cold war days. Russia launched the world's first satellite, SPUTNIK into the space on 4th October, 1957. This was clearly the victory of Russia over the cyber space and as a counter step, Advanced Research Projects Agency, the research arm of Department of Defence, United States, declared the launch of ARPANET (Advanced Research Projects Agency Network) in early 1960"s. This was an experimental network and was designed to keep the computers connected to this network to communicate with each other even if any of the node, due to the bomb attack, fails to respond. The first message was sent over the ARPANET, a packet switching network, by Leonard Kleinrock's laboratory at University of California, Los Angeles (UCLA). You will be surprised to know that the first message that was sent over internet was "LO". Actually, they intended to send word "LOGIN" and only the first two letters reached its destination at second network node at Stanford Research Institute (SRI) and before the last three letters could reach the destination the network was down due to glitch. Soon the error was fixed and the message was resent and it.

The major task that ARPANET had to play is to develop rules for communication i.e., protocols for communicating over ARPANET. The ARPANET in particular led to the development of protocols for internetworking, in which multiple separate networks could be joined into a network of networks. It resulted in the development of TCP/IP protocol suite, which specifies the rules for joining and communicating over ARPANET.

Soon after, in 1986 NSF (national Science Foundation) backbone was created, and five US universities" computing centres were connected to form NSFnet. The participating Universities were:

- Princeton University – John von Neumann National Supercomputer Center, JvNC
- Cornell University – Cornell Theory Center, CTC
- University of Illinois at Urbana-Champaign – National Center for Supercomputing Applications, NCSA
- Carnegie Mellon University – Pittsburgh Supercomputer Center, PSC
- General Atomics – San Diego Supercomputer Center, SDSC

NFSnet, the successor of ARPAnet, became popular by 1990 and ARPANET was decommissioned. There were many parallel networks developed by other Universities and other countries like United Kingdom. In 1965, National Physical Laboratory (NPL) proposed a packet switching network. Michigan Educational Research Information Triad formed MERIT network in 1966 which was funded and supported by State of Michigan and the

National Science Foundation (NSF). France also developed a packet switching network, known as CYCLADES in 1973.

Now there were many parallel systems working on different protocols and the scientists were looking for some common standard so that the networks could be interconnected. In 1978, TCP/IP protocol suites were ready and by 1983, the TCP/IP protocol were adopted by ARPANET.

In 1981, the integration of two large network took place. NFS developed Computer Science Network (CSNET) and was connected to ARPANET using TCP/IP protocol suite. Now the network was not only popular among the research community but the private players also took interest in the network. Initially NFS supported speed of 56 kbit/s. It was upgraded to 1.5 Mbit/s in 1988 to facilitate the growth of network by involving merit network, IBM, MCI and the state of Michigan.

After the corporations took realized the strength and merit of this network, they participated in the development of the network to reap its benefits. By late 1980s many Internet Service Providers (ISPs) emerged to provide the backbone for carrying the network traffic. By 1991, NFSNET was expanded and was upgraded to 45Mbit/s. Many commercial ISPs provided backbone services and was popular among the corporate. To facilitate the commercial use of the network, NFSNET was decommissioned in 1995 and now the Internet could carry commercial traffic.

Now more and more Universities and research centres throughout the world connected to it. Now this network was very popular among the research community and in 1991 National Research and Education Network (NREN) was founded and the World Wide Web was released. Initially the role of internet was only limited to file transfer. The credit of internet what we see it today goes to Tim Berners-Lee who introduced www. With the advent of www, there was a transformation on how the network was used. Now this web of information can be used to retrieve any information available over the internet. Software called; browser was developed to browse the internet. It was developed by researchers at University of Illinois in 1992 and named as Mosaic. This browser enables to browse the internet the way we browse it today.

Internet Addresses

With so many devices connected to the internet, we require some mechanism to uniquely identify every device that is connected to the internet. Also, we require some centralized system which takes care of this mechanism so that the signs which are used to identify each device are not duplicate; else the whole purpose is defeated. To take care of this, we have a centralized authority known as Internet Assigned Numbers Authority (IANA), which is responsible for assigning a unique number known as IP (Internet Protocol) address. An IP address is a 32-bit binary number which is divided into four octets and each octet consists of 8 binary digits and these octets are separated by a dot(.). An example of an IP address is 11110110.01011010.10011100.1111100

Each 8-bits in an octet can have two binary values i.e., 0 and 1. Therefore, each octet can have minimum value 0. i.e., 00000000 to maximum value 255 i.e., 11111111 and in total have 2^8=256 different combinations.

Again, to remember this 32-bit address in binary is bit difficult, so for the better understanding of the human being, it is expressed in a decimal format. But this decimal format is for human understanding only and the computer understands it in binary format only. In decimal, the above IP address is expressed as 123.45.78.125

These octets are used to create and separate different classes. An IP address consists of two parts viz. Network and Host. Network part identifies the network different network and the host part identifies a device of a particular network.

This address uniquely identifies a device connected to the internet similar to the postal system where we identify any house by first identifying the county, then state, district, post office, cluster/block and finally the house number. These IP addresses are classified into five categories based on the availability of IP range. These categories/classes are:

Table 1.1 IP Address Classes

Class	Address range	Supports
Class A	1.0.0.1 to 126.255.255.254	Supports 16 million hosts on each of 127 networks.
Class B	128.1.0.1 to 191.255.255.254	Supports 65,000 hosts on each of 16,000 networks.
Class C	192.0.1.1 to 223.255.254.254	Supports 254 hosts on each of 2 million networks
Class D	224.0.0.0 to 239.255.255.255	Reserved for multicast groups
Class E	240.0.0.0 to 254.255.255.254	Reserved for future use, or Research and Development Purposes.

IANA decentralizes that task of assigning the IP addresses by allocating the large chunk of IP addresses to five Regional Internet Registries (RIRs), which are further responsible to allocate the IP addresses in their zone. These RIRs along with their area of operations are listed below:

APNIC – This RIR is responsible for serving the Asia Pacific region

AFNIC – This RIR is responsible for serving the African region

ARIN – This RIR is responsible for serving North America and several Caribbean and North Atlantic islands

LACNIC – This RIR is responsible for serving Latin America and the Caribbean, and

RIPE NCC – This RIR is responsible for serving Europe, the Middle East, and parts of Central Asia

For liaison and coordinating between these five RIRs, there is an organization called Number Resource Organization (NRO). These organizations are

DNS

Whenever we browse any website in the internet, we type name something like www.uou.ac.in and we rarely deal with IP address like 104.28.2.92 but the fact is even if we type http:\\104.28.2.92 in the URL, it will land us to the same webpage. The fact is we are very comfortable using and remembering the names instead of a number. Moreover, these IP address changes over time and some of the sites have multiple IP address. Also, the transfer of the data over internet is only possible using IP addresses because the routing of the packet of data sent over internet is done using IP address. There is a server called Domain Name System (DNS) which take cares of this translation job to simplify and to save us from remembering these changing IP address numbers, the DNS. Whenever you type an address like http:\\www.uou.ac.in, there is a process called DNS name resolution, takes place in the background. The computer keeps the track of recently visited sites and locally maintains a database in DNS cache. In case, the IP address of the site you have requested for is not found in the DNS cache of your local computer, then the next probable place to find it is DNS server of your Internet Service Provider (ISP). These DNS servers of ISP also maintain the cache of the recently visited pages. Just in case, the information is not found here also, the DNS server of the ISP forward the query to the root nameservers. The root name servers publish the root zone file to other DNS servers and clients on the Internet. The root zone file describes where the authoritative servers for the DNS top-level domains (TLD) are located. There are currently 13 root name servers. They are:

A – VeriSign Global Registry Services

B – University of Southern California – Information Sciences Institute

C – Cogent Communications

D – University of Maryland

E – NASA Ames Research Center

F – Internet Systems Consortium, Inc.

G – U.S. DOD Network Information Center

H – U.S. Army Research Lab

I – Autonomic/NORDUnet

J – VeriSign Global Registry Services

K – RIPE NCC

L – ICANN

M – WIDE Project

These root nameservers directs the query to the appropriate Top-Level Domain(TLD) nameservers by reading the last part of the URL first. In our example the url was http:\\www.uou.ac.in. The last part is .in. Some of the examples of TLD name servers are .com, .biz, .org, .us, .in, etc. These TLD nameservers acts as a switchboard and direct the query to the appropriate authoritative nameserver maintained by each domain. These authoritative nameserver maintains DNS records along with other useful information. This address record is returned back to the requesting host computer via TLD nameservers, nameservers, ISP"s DNS server. These intermediate server keeps the record of this IP address in their DNS cache, so that if the same request is encountered again, they don't have to go through this process again. If the same URL is requested again, the DNS cache of the local host computer will return the IP address of the URL.

Internet Infrastructure

Internet, as the name suggests, in a network of network i.e. it is a collection of several small, medium and large networks. This clearly indicates to one fact, nobody is a single owner of the internet and it is one of the proven example of collaborative success. Now you must be surprised how such a large network which is spread across the continents can run without the any problem. Yes it is correct that to monitor such a large network, we require an international body which can frame the rules, regulation and protocols to join and use this network. Therefore, an international organization, known as "The Internet Society" was formed in 1992 to take care of such issues.

Let us now discuss, how this internet works? How the email you sent to your friend is received by your friend's computer located at another country/continent. When you are working in your laptop/desktop in your home without connecting to the internet, your computer is a standalone system. But, whenever you connect to the internet by dialing to your Internet Service Provider(ISP) using your modem, you become the part of the network. The ISP is the link between the internet backbone, through which the entire data route, and the user. The ISP connects to the internet backbone at Network Access Points(NAP). These NAPs are the provided by the large telecommunication companies at various regions. These large telecommunication companies connect the countries and the continents by building and maintaining the large backbone infrastructure to route data from NAP to NAP. ISPs are connected to this backbone at NAP and are responsible build and manage network locally. So when you dial internet through modem, you first become part of the local ISP, which in turn connects to the internet backbone through NAP. The data is routed through this backbone and sent to the destination NAP, where the ISP of your friend's network is located. As soon as your friend dials his modem to connect to the internet, the data is delivered to your friend's computer.

World Wide Web

Sometimes we interchangeably use the term internet and world wide web or simply the web, as it is popularly known as. But web is only one of the several the utilities that internet provides. Some of the popular service that internet provides other then web is e-mail, usenet, messaging service, FTP, etc. The web use HTTP protocol to communicate over internet and to exchange information. The web was developed at CERN (Europeen de Reserches Nucleaires), Switzerland) by a UK scientist Tim Berners-

Lee in 1989. It consists of all the public web sites and all the devices that access the web content. WWW is an information sharing model which is developed to exchange information over the internet. There are plenty of public websites, which is a collection of web pages, available over the internet. These web – pages contain plenty of information in a form of text, videos, audio and picture format. These web pages are access using a application software called a web browser. Some of the examples of the popular web browser are: Internet explorer, Chrome, Safari, Firefox, etc.

So this was a little introduction about internet and how it functions. Now let us discuss about cybercrime.

1.2 Introduction to Cyber Crime

The internet was born around 1960"s where its access was limited to few scientist, researchers and the defence only. Internet user base has evolved exponentially. Initially the computer crime was only confined to making a physical damage to the computer and related infrastructure. Around 1980"s the trend changed from causing the physical damaging to computers to making a computer malfunction using a malicious code called virus. Till then the effect was not so widespread because internet was only confined to defence setups, large international companies and research communities. In 1996, when internet was launched for the public, it immediately became popular among the masses and they slowly became dependent on it to an extent that it have changed their lifestyle. The GUIs were written so well that the user don't have to bother how the internet was functioning. They have to simply make few click over the hyper-links or type the desired information at the desired place without bothering where this data is stored and how it is sent over the internet or whether the data can accessed by another person who is connected to the internet or whether the data packet sent over the internet can be spoofed and tampered. The focus of the computer crime shifted from merely damaging the computer or destroying or manipulating data for personal benefit to financial crime. These computer attacks are increasing at a rapid pace. Every second around 25 computer became victim to cyber-attack and around 800 million individuals are affected by it till 2013. CERT-India have reported around 308371 Indian websites to be hacked between 2011-2013. It is also estimated that around $160 million are lost per year due to cyber-crime. This figure is very conservative as most of the cases are never reported.

According to the 2013-14 report of the standing committee on Information Technology to the 15th Lok Sabha by ministry of communication and information technology, India has the third-largest number of Internet users throughout the world with an estimated 100 million internet users as on June, 2011 and the numbers are growing rapidly. There are around 22 million broadband connections in India till date operated by around 134 major Internet Service Providers(ISPs).

Before discussing the matter further, let us know what the cyber crime is?

The term cyber crime is used to describe an unlawful activity in which computer or computing devices such as smartphones, tablets, Personal Digital Assistants(PDAs), etc. which are stand alone or a part of a network are used as a tool or/and target of criminal activity. It is often committed by the people of destructive and criminal mindset either for revenge, greed or adventure.

1.2.1 Classification of Cyber Crimes

The cyber-criminal could be internal or external to the organization facing the cyber-attack. Based on this fact, the cyber-crime could be categorized into two types:

Insider Attack: An attack to the network or the computer system by some person with authorized system access is known as insider attack. It is generally performed by dissatisfied or unhappy inside employees or contractors. The motive of the insider attack could be revenge or greed. It is comparatively easy for an insider to perform a cyber-attack as he is well aware of the policies, processes, IT architecture and weakness of the security system. Moreover, the attacker have an access to the network. Therefore, it is comparatively easy for a insider attacker to steel sensitive information, crash the network, etc. In most of the cases the reason for insider attack is when a employee is fired or assigned new roles in an organization, and the role is not reflected in the IT policies. This opens a vulnerability window for the attacker. The insider attack could be prevented by planning and installing an Internal intrusion detection system (IDS) in the organization.

External Attack: When the attacker is either hired by an insider or an external entity to the organization, it is known as external attack. The organization which is a victim of cyber-attack not only faces financial loss but also the loss of reputation. Since the attacker is external to the organization, so these attackers usually scan and gathering information. An experienced network/security administrator keeps regular eye on the log generated by the firewalls as external attacks can be traced out by carefully analyzing these firewall logs. Also, Intrusion Detection Systems are installed to keep an eye on external attacks.

The cyber-attacks can also be classified as structure attacks and unstructured attacks based on the level of maturity of the attacker. Some of the authors have classified these attacks as a form of external attacks but there is precedence of the cases when a structured attack was performed by an internal employee. This happens in the case when the competitor company wants the future strategy of an organization on certain points. The attacker may strategically gain access to the company as an employee and access the required information.

Unstructured attacks: These attacks are generally performed by amateurs who don"t have any predefined motives to perform the cyber-attack. Usually, these amateurs try to test a tool readily available over the internet on the network of a random company.

Structure Attack: These types of attacks are performed by highly skilled and experienced people and the motives of these attacks are clear in their mind. They have access to sophisticated tools and technologies to gain access to other networks without being noticed by their Intrusion Detection Systems(IDSs). Moreover, these attackers have the necessary expertise to develop or modify the existing tools to satisfy their purpose. These types of attacks are usually performed by professional criminals, by a country on other rival countries, politicians to damage the image of the rival person or the country, terrorists, rival companies, etc.

Cyber-crimes have turned out to be a low-investment, low-risk business with huge returns. Now-a-days these structured crimes are performed are highly organized. There is a perfect hierarchical organizational setup like formal organizations and some of them have reached a level in technical capabilities at par with those of developed nation. They are targeting large financial organizations, defence and nuclear establishments and they are also into online drugs trading.

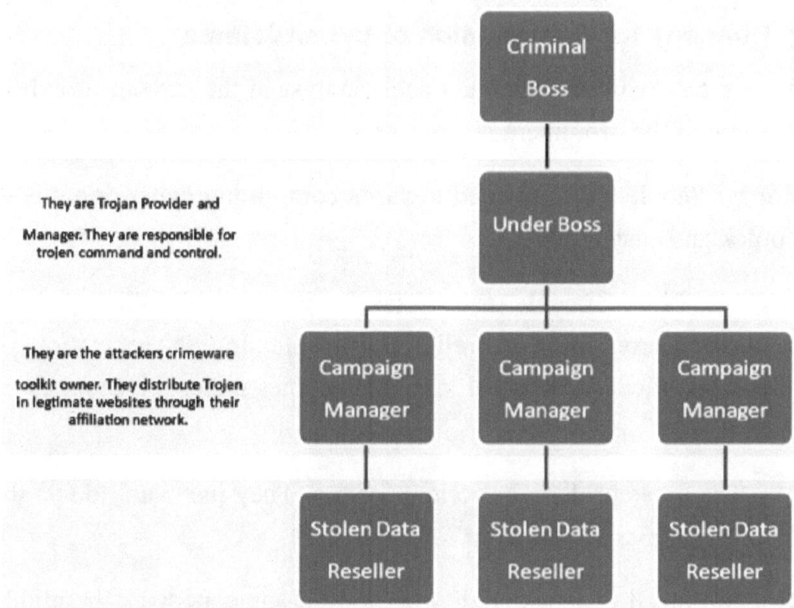

Figure 1.1: Hierarchical Organizational Structure

Hierarchical Organizational Structure is shown in figure 1. The role of all the people in the hierarchy remain changing and it is based on the opportunity. If a hacker who have hacked sensitive data from an organization may use it for financially exploiting the organization himself. In case, the hacker himself have the technical expertise for it, he will do it himself, otherwise he may find a buyer who is interested in that data and have the technical expertise.

There are some cyber criminals offers on-demand and service. The person, organization or a country may contact these cyber criminals for hacking an organization to gain access to some sensitive data, or create massive denial-of –service attack on their competitors. Based on the demand of the customer the hackers write malware, virus, etc. to suit their requirements. An organization effected by a cyber-attack, not only faces financial loss, but its reputation is also adversely affected, and the competitor organization will defiantly benefit by it.

1.2.2 Reasons for Commission of Cyber Crimes

There are many reasons which act as a catalyst in the growth of cyber-crime. Some of the prominent reasons are:

Money: People are motivated towards committing cyber-crime is to make quick and easy money.

Revenge: Some people try to take revenge with other person/ organization/society/ caste or religion by defaming its reputation or bringing economical or physical loss. This comes under the category of cyber terrorism.

Fun: The amateur do cyber-crime for fun. They just want to test the latest tool they have encountered.

Recognition: It is considered to be pride if someone hack the highly secured networks like defense sites or networks.

Anonymity – Many time the anonymity that a cyber space provide motivates the person to commit cyber-crime as it is much easy to commit a cyber-crime over the cyber space and remain anonymous as compared to real world.

It is much easier to get away with criminal activity in a cyber world than in the real world. There is a strong sense of anonymity than can draw otherwise respectable citizens to abandon their ethics in pursuit personal gain.

Cyber Espionage: At times the government itself is involved in cyber trespassing to keep eye on other person/network/country. The reason could be politically, economically socially motivated.

1.3 Malware and its Type

Malware stands for "Malicious Software" and it is designed to gain access or installed into the computer without the consent of the user. They perform unwanted tasks in the host computer for the benefit of a third party. There is a full range of malwares which can seriously degrade the performance of the host machine. Also these are simply written to distract/annoy the user, to the complex ones which captures the sensitive data from the host machine and send it to remote servers. There are various types of malwares present in the Internet. Some of the popular ones are:

1.3.1 Adware

It is a special type of malware which is used for forced advertising. They either redirect the page to some advertising page or pop-up an additional page which promotes some product or event. This adware is financially supported by the organizations whose products are advertised.

1.3.2 Spyware

It is a special type of which is installed in the target computer with or without the user permission and is designed to steal sensitive information from the target machine. Mostly it gathers the browsing habits of the user and the send it to the remote server without the knowledge of the owner of the computer. Most of the time they are downloaded in to the host computer while downloading freeware i.e. free application programs from the internet. Spywares may be of various types; It can keep track of the cookies of the host computer, it can act as a keyloggers to sniff the banking passwords and sensitive information, etc.

1.3.3 Browser Hijacking Software

There is some malicious software which are downloaded along with the free software offered over the internet and installed in the host computer without the knowledge of the user. This software modifies the browsers setting and redirect links to other unintentional sites.

1.3.4 Virus

A virus is a malicious code written to damage/harm the host computer by deleting or appending a file, occupy memory space of the computer by replicating the copy of the code, slow down the performance of the computer, format the host machine, etc. It can be spread via email attachment, pen drives, digital images, e-greeting, audio or video clips, etc. A virus may be present in a computer but it cannot activate itself without the human intervention.

Until and unless the executable file(.exe) is execute, a virus cannot be activated in the host machine.

1.3.5 Worms

They are a class of virus which can replicate themselves. They are different from the virus by the fact that they do not require human intervention to travel over the network and spread from the infected machine to the whole network. Worms can spread either through network, using the loopholes of the Operating System or via email. The replication and spreading of the worm over the network consume the network resources like space and bandwidth and force the network to choke.

1.3.6 Trojan Horse

Trojan horse is a malicious code that is installed in the host machine by pretending to be useful software. The user clicks on the link or download the file which pretends to be a useful file or software from legitimate source. It not only damages the host computer by manipulating the data but also it creates a backdoor in the host computer so that it could be controlled by a remote computer. It can become a part of botnet(robot-network), a network of computers which are infected by malicious code and controlled by central controller. The computers of this network which are infected by malicious code are known as zombies. Trojans neither infect the other computers in the network nor do they replicate. Figure 1.2 shows a typical botnet.

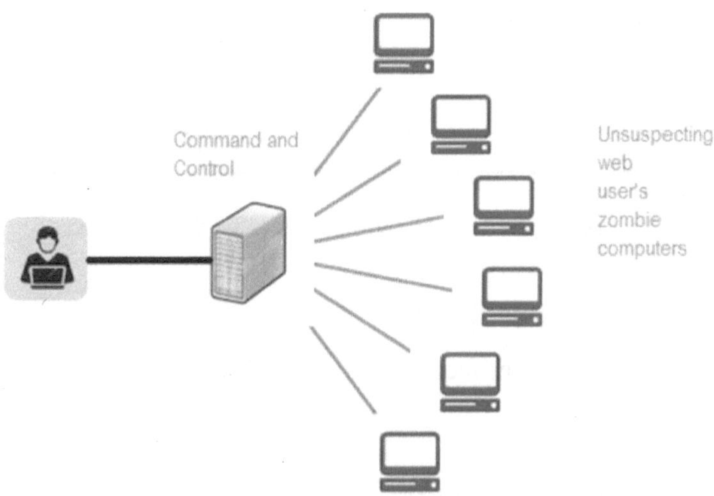

Figure 1.2: A typical botnet

1.3.7 Scareware

Internet has changed how we talk, shop, play etc. It has even changed the way how the criminal target the people for ransom. While surfing the Internet, suddenly a pop-up alert appears in the screen which warns the presence of dangerous virus, spywares, etc. in the user's computer. As a remedial measure, the message suggests the user download the full paid version of the software. As the user proceeds to download, a malicious code, known as scareware is downloaded into the host computer. It holds the host computer hostage until the ransom is paid. The malicious code can neither be uninstalled nor can the computer be used till the ransom is paid. A sample message alert of a scareware is shown below in Figure 1.3.

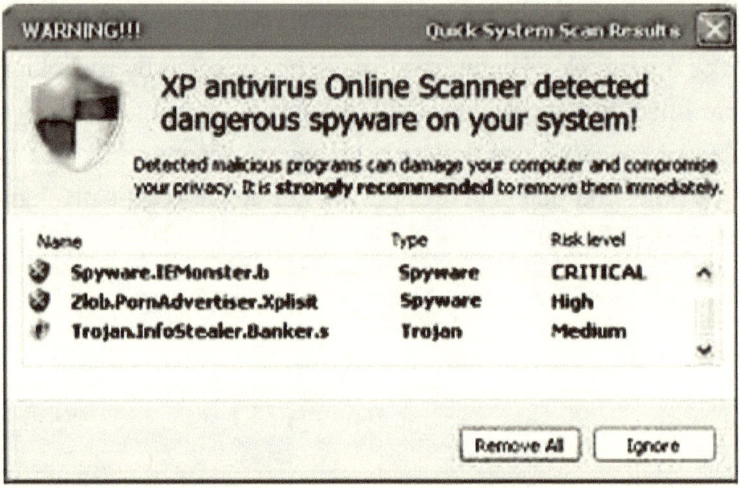

Figure 1.3: Sample Warning Message of a Scareware

1.4 Kinds of Cyber Crime

Various types of cyber-crimes are

Cyber Stalking

It is an act of stalking, harassing or threatening someone using Internet/ computer as a medium. This is often done to defame a person and use email, social network, instant messenger, web-posting, etc. Using Internet as a medium as it offers anonymity. The behavior includes false accusations, threats, sexual exploitation to minors, monitoring, etc.

Child Pornography

It is an act of possessing image or video of a minor (under 18), engaged in sexual conduct.

Forgery and Counterfeiting

It is the use of a computer to forge and counterfeit document. With the advancement in the hardware and the software, it is possible to produce counterfeit which matches the original document to such an extent that it is not possible to judge the authenticity of the document without expert judgement.

Software Piracy and Crime Related to IPRs

Software piracy is an illegal reproduction and distribution for personal use or business. It comes under crime related to IPR infringement. Some of the other crimes under IPR infringement are: download of songs, downloading movies, etc.

Cyber Terrorism

It is defined as the use of computer resources to intimidate or coerce government, the civilian population or any segment thereof in furtherance of political or social objectives.

Phishing

It is a process of acquiring personal and sensitive information of an individual via email by disguising as a trustworthy entity in an electronic communication. The purpose of phishing is identity theft and the personal information like username, password, and credit card number etc. may be used to steal money from user account. If a telephone is used as a medium for identity theft, it is known as Vishing (voice phishing). Another form of phishing is Smishing, in which sms is used to lure customers.

Computer Vandalism

It is an act of physical destroying computing resources using physical force or malicious code.

Computer Hacking

It is a practice of modifying computer hardware and software to accomplish a goal outside the creator's original purpose. The purpose of hacking a computer system may vary from simply demonstrations of the technical ability, to stealing, modifying or destroying information for social, economic or political reasons. Now the corporate is hiring hackers, a person who is engaged in hacking computers, to intentionally hack the computer of an organization to find and fix security vulnerabilities.

The Hackers May Be Classified As

White Hat: white hat hackers are the persons who hack the system to find the security vulnerabilities of a system and notify to the organizations so that a preventive action can be taken to protect the system from outside hackers. White hat hackers may be paid employee of an organization who is employed to find the security loop-holes, or may be a freelancer who just wants to prove his mantle in this field. They are popular known as ethical hackers.

Black Hat: in contrast to the white hat, the black hat hacks the system with ill intentions. They may hack the system for social, political or economically motivated intentions. They find the security loopholes in the system, and keep the information themselves and exploit the system for personal or organizational benefits till organization whose system is compromised is aware of this, and apply security patches. They are popularly known as crackers.

Grey Hat: Grey hat hackers find out the security vulnerabilities and report to the site administrators and offer the fix of the security bug for a consultancy fee.

Blue hat: A blue hat hacker is someone outside computer security consulting firms who is used to bug-test a system prior to its launch, looking for exploits so they can be closed.

Creating and Distributing Viruses Over Internet

The spreading of a virus can cause business and financial loss to an organization. The loss includes the cost of repairing the system, cost associated with the loss of business during downtime and cost of loss of opportunity. The organization can sue the hacker, if found, for the sum of more than or equivalent to the loss borne by the organization.

Spamming

Sending of unsolicited and commercial bulk message over the internet is known as spamming. An email can be classified as spam, if it meets following criteria:

Mass mailing:- the email is not targeted to one particular person but to a large number of peoples.

Anonymity:- The real identify of the person not known

Unsolicited:- the email is neither expected nor requested for the recipient.

These spams not only irritate the recipients and overload the network but also waste the time and occupy the valuable memory space of the mailbox.

Cross Site Scripting

It is an activity which involves injecting a malicious client side script into a trusted website. As soon as the browser executes the malicious script, the malicious script gets access to the cookies and other sensitive information and sent to remote servers. Now this information can be use to gain financial benefit or physical access to a system for personal interest.

Online Auction Fraud

There are many genuine websites who offers online auction over internet. Taking the advantage of the reputation of these websites, some of the cyber criminals lure the customers to online auction fraud schemes which often lead to either overpayment of the product or the item is never delivered once the payment is made.

Cyber Squatting

It is an act of reserving the domain names of someone else's trademark with intent to sell it afterwards to the organization who is the owner of the trademark at a higher price.

Logic Bombs

These are malicious code inserted into legitimate software. The malicious action is triggered by some specific condition. If the conditions holds true in future, the malicious action begins and based on the action defined in the malicious code, they either destroy the information stored in the system or make system unusable.

Web Jacking

The hacker gain access to a website of an organization and either blocks it or modify it to serve political, economical or social interest. The recent examples of web jacking are some of the websites of the educational institutes were hacked by Pakistani hackers and an animation which contains Pakistani flags were flashed in the homepage of these websites. Another example is Indian hackers hacked website of Pakistani railways and flashed Indian flag in the homepage for several hours on the occasion of Independence Day of India in 2014.

Internet Time Thefts

Hacking the username and password of ISP of an individual and surfing the internet at his cost is Internet Time Theft.

Denial of Service Attack

It is a cyber-attack in which the network is chocked and often collapsed by flooding it with useless traffic and thus preventing the legitimate network traffic.

Salami Attack

It is an attack which proceeds with small increments and final add up to lead to a major attack. The increments are so small that they remain unnoticed. An example of salami attack is gaining access to online banking of an individual and withdrawing amount in such a small amounts that it remains unnoticed by the owner. Often there is default trigger set in the banking website and transactions below say, Rs. 1000 withdrawal are not reported to the owner of the account. Withdrawing amount of Rs. 1000 over a period of time will lead to total withdrawal of a large sum.

Data Diddling

It is a practice of changing the data before its entry into the computer system. Often, the original data is retained after the execution on the data is done. For example, DA or the basic salary of the person is changed in the payroll data of an individual for pay calculation. Once the salary is calculated and transferred to his account, the total salary is replaced by his actual salary in the report.

Email Spoofing

It is a process of changing the header information of an e-mail so that its original source is not identified and it appears to an individual at the receiving end that the email has been originated from source other than the original source.

Chapter 2

Cybersecurity Techniques

There are many cyber security techniques to combat the cyber security attacks. The next section discusses some of the popular techniques to counter the cyber-attacks.

2.1 Authentication

It is a process of identifying an individual and ensuring that the individual is the same who he/she claims to be. A typical method for authentication over internet is via username and password. With the increase in the reported cases of cyber-crime by identity theft over internet, the organizations have made some additional arrangements for authentication like One Time Password(OTP), as the name suggest it is a password which can be used one time only and is sent to the user as an SMS or an email at the mobile number/email address that he have specified during the registration process. It is known as two-factor authentication method and requires two type of evidence to authentication an individual to provide an extra layer of security for authentication. Some other popular techniques for two-factor authentication(2FA) are: biometric data, physical token, etc. which are used in conjunction with username and password.

The authentication becomes more important in light of the fact that today the multinational organizations have changed the way the business was to be say, 15 years back. They have offices present around the Globe, and an employee may want an access which is present in a centralized sever. Or an employee is working from home and not using the office intranet and wants an access to some particular file present in the office network. The system needs to authenticate the user and based on the credentials of that user, may or may not provide access to the user to the information he requested. The process of giving access to an individual to certain resources based on the credentials of an individual is known as authorization and often this process goes hand-in-hand with authentication. Now, one can easily understand the role of strong password for authorization to ensure cyber security as an easy password can be a cause of security flaw and can bring the whole organization at high risk. Therefore, the password policy of an organization should be such that employees are forced to use strong passwords (more than 12 characters and combination of lowercase and uppercase alphabets along with numbers and special characters) and prompt user to change their password frequently. In some of the bigger organizations or an organization which deals in sensitive information like defence agencies, financial institutions, planning commissions, etc. a hybrid authentication system is used which combines both the username and password along with hardware security measures like biometric system, etc. Some of the larger organizations also use VPN(Virtual Private Network), which is one of the method to provide secure access via hybrid security authentication to the company network over internet.

2.2 Encryption

It is a technique to convert the data in unreadable form before transmitting it over the internet. Only the person who have the access to the key and convert it in the readable form and read it. Formally encryption can be defined as a technique to lock the data by converting it to complex codes using mathematical algorithms. The code is so complex that even the most powerful computer will take several years to break the code. This secure code can safely be transmitted over internet to the destination. The receiver, after receiving the data can decode it using the key. The decoding of the complex code to original text using key is known as decryption. If the same key is used to lock and unlock the data, it is known as symmetric key encryption and it is shown in figure 2.1.

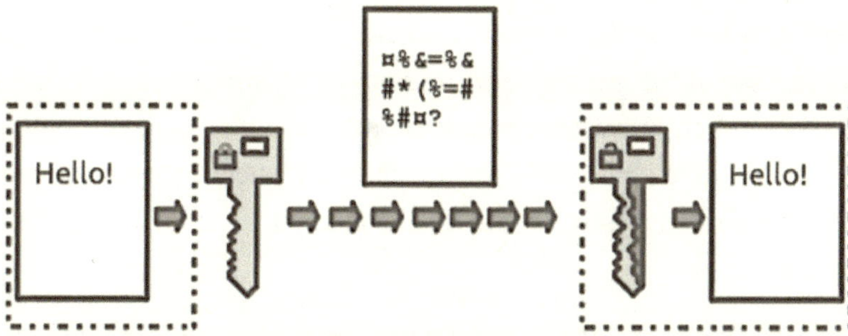

Figure 2.1: Encryption

In symmetric key encryption, the after coding of data, the key is sent to the destination user via some other medium like postal service, telephone, etc. because if the key obtained by the hacker, the security of the data is compromised. Key distribution is a complex task because the security of key while transmission is itself an issue. To avoid the transfer of key a method called asymmetric key encryption, also known as public key encryption, is used. In asymmetric key encryption, the key used to encrypt and decrypt data are different. Every user possesses two keys viz. public key and private key. As the name suggest, the public key of every user is known to everyone but the private key is known to the particular user, who own the key, only. Suppose sender A wants to send a secret message to receiver B through internet. A will encrypt the message using B"s public key, as the public key is known to everyone. Once the message is encrypted, the message can safely be sent to B over internet. As soon as the message is received by B, he will use his private key to decrypt the message and regenerate the original message.

2.2.1 History

1. Ancient

One of the earliest forms of encryption is symbol replacement, which was first found in the tomb of Khnumhotep II, who lived in 1900 BC

Egypt. Symbol replacement encryption is "non-standard," which means that the symbols require a cipher or key to understand. This type of early encryption was used throughout Ancient Greece and Rome for military purposes. One of the most famous military encryption developments was the Caesar cipher, in which a plaintext letter is shifted a fixed number of positions along the alphabet to get the encoded letter. A message encoded with this type of encryption could be decoded with a fixed number on the Caesar cipher.

Around 800 AD, Arab mathematician Al-Kindi developed the technique of frequency analysis – which was an attempt to crack ciphers systematically, including the Caesar cipher. This technique looked at the frequency of letters in the encrypted message to determine the appropriate shift: for example, the most common letter in English text is E and is therefore likely to be represented by the letter that appears most commonly in the ciphertext. This technique was rendered ineffective by the polyalphabetic cipher, described by Al-Qalqashandi (1355–1418) and Leon Battista Alberti (in 1465), which varied the substitution alphabet as encryption proceeded in order to confound such analysis.

2. 19th–20th Century

Around 1790, Thomas Jefferson theorized a cipher to encode and decode messages to provide a more secure way of military correspondence. The cipher, known today as the Wheel Cipher or the Jefferson Disk, although never actually built, was theorized as a spool that could jumble an English message up to 36 characters. The message could be decrypted by plugging in the jumbled message to a receiver with an identical cipher.

A similar device to the Jefferson Disk, the M-94, was developed in 1917 independently by US Army Major Joseph Mauborne. This device was used in U.S. military communications until 1942.

In World War II, the Axis powers used a more advanced version of the M-94 called the Enigma Machine. The Enigma Machine was more complex because unlike the Jefferson Wheel and the M-94, each day the jumble of letters switched to a completely new combination. Each day's combination was only known by the Axis, so many thought the only way to break the code would be to try over 17,000 combinations within 24 hours. The Allies used computing power to severely limit the number of reasonable combinations they needed to check every day, leading to the breaking of the Enigma Machine.

3. Modern

Today, encryption is used in the transfer of communication over the Internet for security and commerce. As computing power continues to increase, computer encryption is constantly evolving to prevent eavesdropping attacks. One of the first "modern" cipher suites, DES, used a 56-bit key with 72,057,594,037,927,936 possibilities; it was cracked in 1999 by EFF's brute-force DES cracker, which required 22 hours and 15 minutes to do so. Modern encryption standards often use stronger key sizes, such as AES (256-bit mode), TwoFish, ChaCha20-Poly1305, Serpent (configurable up to 512-bit). Cipher suites that use a 128-bit or higher key, like AES, will not be able to be brute-forced because the total amount of keys is 3.4028237e+38 possibilities. The most likely option for cracking ciphers with high key size is to find vulnerabilities in the cipher itself, like inherent biases and backdoors or by exploiting physical side effects through Side-channel attacks. For example, RC4, a stream cipher, was cracked due to inherent biases and vulnerabilities in the cipher.

4. Encryption in Cryptography

In the context of cryptography, encryption serves as a mechanism to ensure confidentiality. Since data may be visible on the Internet, sensitive information such as passwords and personal communication may be exposed to potential interceptors. The process of encrypting and decrypting messages involves keys. The two main types of keys in cryptographic systems are symmetric-key and public-key (also known as asymmetric-key).

Many complex cryptographic algorithms often use simple modular arithmetic in their implementations.

5. Types

In symmetric-key schemes, the encryption and decryption keys are the same. Communicating parties must have the same key in order to achieve secure communication. The German Enigma Machine used a new symmetric-key each day for encoding and decoding messages.

In public-key cryptography schemes, the encryption key is published for anyone to use and encrypt messages. However, only the receiving party has access to the decryption key that enables messages to be read. Public-key encryption was first described in a secret document in 1973; beforehand, all encryption schemes were symmetric-key (also called private-key). Although published subsequently, the work of Diffie and Hellman was published in a journal with a large readership, and the value of the methodology was explicitly described. The method became known as the Diffie-Hellman key exchange.

RSA (Rivest–Shamir–Adleman) is another notable public-key cryptosystem. Created in 1978, it is still used today for applications involving digital signatures. Using number theory, the RSA algorithm selects two prime numbers, which help generate both the encryption and decryption keys.

A publicly available public-key encryption application called Pretty Good Privacy (PGP) was written in 1991 by Phil Zimmermann, and distributed free of charge with source code. PGP was purchased by Symantec in 2010 and is regularly updated.

6. Uses

Encryption has long been used by militaries and governments to facilitate secret communication. It is now commonly used in protecting information within many kinds of civilian systems. For example, the Computer Security Institute reported that in 2007, 71% of companies surveyed used encryption for some of their data in transit, and 53% used encryption for some of their data in storage. Encryption can be used to protect data "at rest", such as information stored on computers and storage devices (e.g. USB flash drives). In recent years, there have been numerous reports of confidential data, such as customers' personal records, being exposed through loss or theft of laptops or backup drives; encrypting such files at rest helps protect them if physical security measures fail. Digital rights management systems, which prevent unauthorized use or reproduction of copyrighted material and protect software against reverse engineering (see also copy protection), is another somewhat different example of using encryption on data at rest.

Encryption is also used to protect data in transit, for example data being transferred via networks (e.g. the Internet, e-commerce), mobile telephones, wireless microphones, wireless intercom systems, Bluetooth devices and bank automatic teller machines. There have been numerous reports of data in transit being intercepted in recent years. Data should also be encrypted when transmitted across networks in order to protect against eavesdropping of network traffic by unauthorized users.

7. Data Erasure

Conventional methods for permanently deleting data from a storage device involve overwriting the device's whole content with zeros, ones, or other patterns – a process which can take a significant amount of time, depending on the capacity and the type of storage medium. Cryptography offers a way of making the erasure almost instantaneous. This method is called crypto-shredding. An example implementation of this method can be found on iOS devices, where the cryptographic key is kept in a dedicated 'effaceable storage'. Because the key is stored on the same device, this setup on its own does not offer full privacy or security protection if an unauthorized person gains physical access to the device.

8. Limitations

Encryption is used in the 21st century to protect digital data and information systems. As computing power increased over the years, encryption technology has only become more advanced and secure. However, this advancement in technology has also exposed a potential limitation of today's encryption methods.

The length of the encryption key is an indicator of the strength of the encryption method. For example, the original encryption key, DES (Data Encryption Standard), was 56 bits, meaning it had 2^56 combination possibilities. With today's computing power, a 56-bit key is no longer secure, being vulnerable to brute force attacks.

Quantum computing uses properties of quantum mechanics in order to process large amounts of data simultaneously. Quantum computing has been found to achieve computing speeds thousands of times faster than today's supercomputers. This computing power presents a challenge to today's encryption technology. For example, RSA encryption uses the multiplication of very large prime numbers to create a semiprime number for its public key. Decoding this key without its private key requires this semiprime number to be factored, which can take a very long time to do with modern computers. It would take a supercomputer anywhere between weeks to months to factor in this key. However, quantum computing can use quantum algorithms to factor this semiprime number in the same amount of time it takes for normal computers to generate it. This would make all data protected by current public-key encryption vulnerable to quantum computing attacks. Other encryption techniques like elliptic curve cryptography and symmetric key encryption are also vulnerable to quantum computing.

While quantum computing could be a threat to encryption security in the future, quantum computing as it currently stands is still very limited. Quantum computing currently is not commercially available, cannot handle large amounts of code, and only exists as computational devices, not computers. Furthermore, quantum computing advancements will be able to be used in favor of encryption as well. The National Security Agency (NSA) is currently preparing post-quantum encryption standards for the future. Quantum encryption promises a level of security that will be able to counter the threat of quantum computing.

9. Attacks and Countermeasures

Encryption is an important tool but is not sufficient alone to ensure the security or privacy of sensitive information throughout its lifetime. Most applications of encryption protect information only at rest or in transit, leaving sensitive data in clear text and potentially vulnerable to improper disclosure during processing, such as by a cloud service for example. Homomorphic encryption and secure multi-party computation are emerging techniques to compute encrypted data; these techniques are general and Turing complete but incur high computational and/or communication costs.

In response to encryption of data at rest, cyber-adversaries have developed new types of attacks. These more recent threats to encryption of data at rest include cryptographic attacks, stolen ciphertext attacks, attacks on encryption keys, insider attacks, data corruption or integrity attacks, data destruction attacks, and ransomware attacks. Data fragmentation and active defense data protection technologies attempt to counter some of these attacks, by distributing, moving, or mutating ciphertext so it is more difficult to identify, steal, corrupt, or destroy.

10. The Debate Around Encryption

The question of balancing the need for national security with the right to privacy has been debated for years, since encryption has become critical in today's digital society. The modern encryption debate started around the '90s when US government tried to ban cryptography because, according to them, it would threaten national security. The debate is polarized around two opposing views. Those who see strong encryption as a problem making it easier for criminals to hide their illegal acts online and others who argue that encryption keep digital communications safe. The debate heated up in 2014, when Big Tech like Apple and Google set encryption by default in their devices. This was the start of a series of controversies that puts governments, companies and internet users at stake.

11. Integrity Protection of Ciphertexts

Encryption, by itself, can protect the confidentiality of messages, but other techniques are still needed to protect the integrity and authenticity of a message; for example, verification of a message authentication code (MAC) or a digital signature usually done by a hashing algorithm or a PGP signature. Authenticated encryption algorithms are designed to provide both encryption and integrity protection together. Standards for cryptographic software and hardware to perform encryption are widely available, but successfully using encryption to ensure security may be a challenging problem. A single error in system design or execution can allow successful attacks. Sometimes an adversary can obtain unencrypted information without directly undoing the encryption. See for example traffic analysis, TEMPEST, or Trojan horse.

Integrity protection mechanisms such as MACs and digital signatures must be applied to the ciphertext when it is first created, typically on the same device used to compose the message, to protect a message end-to-end along its full transmission path; otherwise, any node between the sender and the encryption agent could potentially tamper with it. Encrypting at the time of creation is only secure if the encryption device itself has correct keys and has not been tampered with. If an endpoint device has been configured to trust a root certificate that an attacker controls, for example, then the attacker can both inspect and tamper with encrypted data by performing a man-in-the-middle attack anywhere along the message's path. The common practice of TLS interception by network operators represents a controlled and institutionally sanctioned form of such an attack, but countries have also attempted to employ such attacks as a form of control and censorship.

12. Ciphertext Length and Padding

Even when encryption correctly hides a message's content and it cannot be tampered with at rest or in transit, a message's length is a form of metadata that can still leak sensitive information about the message. For example, the well-known CRIME and BREACH attacks against HTTPS were side-channel attacks that relied on information leakage via the length of encrypted content. Traffic analysis is a broad class of techniques that often employs message lengths to infer sensitive implementation about traffic flows by aggregating information about a large number of messages.

Padding a message's payload before encrypting it can help obscure the cleartext's true length, at the cost of increasing the ciphertext's size and introducing or increasing bandwidth overhead. Messages may be padded randomly or deterministically, with each approach having different tradeoffs. Encrypting and padding messages to form padded uniform random blobs or PURBs is a practice guaranteeing that the cipher text leaks no metadata about its cleartext's content, and leaks asymptotically minimal information via its length.

2.3 Digital Signatures

It is a technique for validation of data. Validation is a process of certifying the content of a document. The digital signatures not only validate the data but also used for authentication. The digital signature is created by encrypting the data with the private key of the sender. The encrypted data is attached along with the original message and sent over the internet to the destination. The receiver can decrypt the signature with the public key of the sender. Now the decrypted message is compared with the original message. If both are same, it signifies that the data is not tampered and also the authenticity of the sender is verified as someone with the private key(which is known to the owner only) can encrypt the data which was then decrypted by his public key. If the data is tampered while transmission, it is easily detected by the receiver as the data will not be verified. Moreover, the massage cannot be re-encrypted after tempering as the private key, which is posses only by the original sender, is required for this purpose.

As more and more documents are transmitted over internet, digital signatures shown in figure 2.2 are essential part of the legal as well as the financial transition. It not only provides the authentication of a person and the validation of the document, it also prevents the denial or agreement at a later stage. Suppose a shareholder instructs the broker via email to sell the share at the current price. After the completion of the transaction, by any chance, the shareholder reclaims the shares by claiming the email to be forge or bogus. To prevent these unpleasant situations, the digital signatures are used.

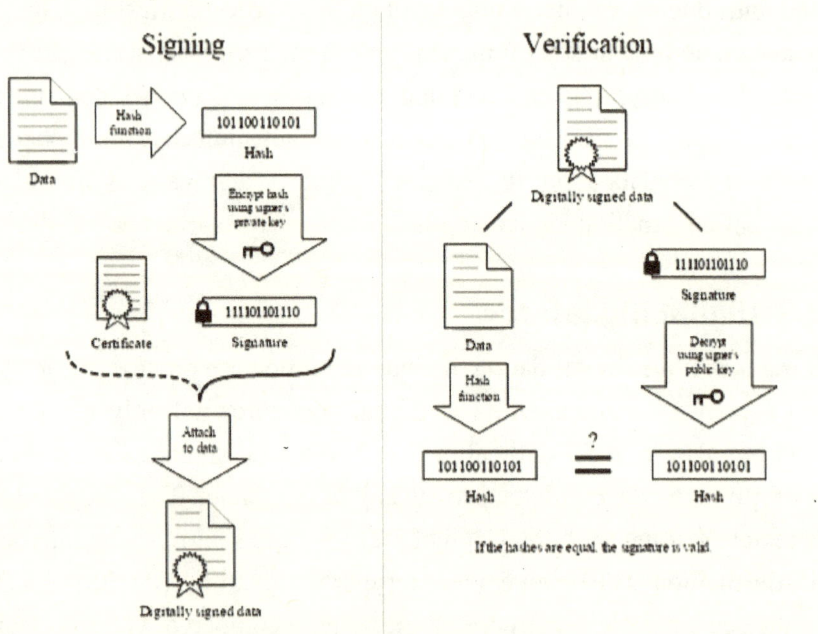

Figure 2.2: Digital signature

2.4 Antivirus

There are varieties of malicious programs like virus, worms, trojan horse, etc that are spread over internet to compromise the security of a computer either to destroy data stored into the computer or gain financial benefits by sniffing passwords etc and these are shown in figure 2.3. To prevent these malicious codes to enter to your system, a special program called an anti-virus is used which is designed to protect the system against virus. It not only prevents the malicious code to enter the system but also detect and destroy the malicious code that is already installed into the system. There are lots of new viruses coming every day. The antivirus program regularly updates its database and provides immunity to the system against these new viruses, worms, etc.

Figure 2.3: Different antivirus available on the market

2.5 Firewall

It is a hardware/software which acts as a shield between an organization"s network and the internet and protects it from the threats like virus, malware, hackers, etc. It can be used to limit the persons who can have access to your network and send information to you and it is shown in figure 2.4.

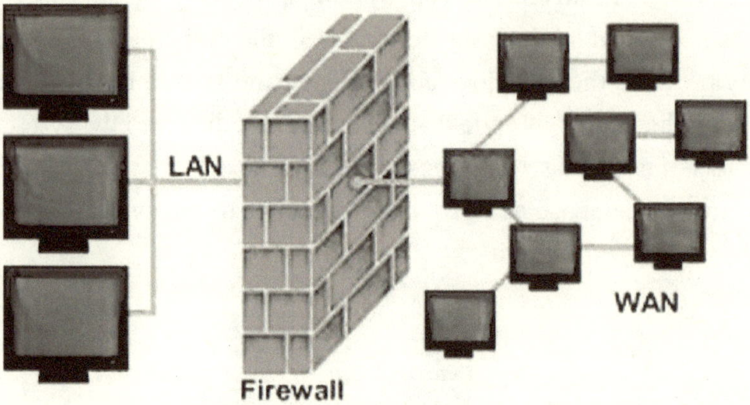

Figure 2.4: Firewall

There are two types of traffic in an organization viz. inbound traffic and outbound traffic. Using firewall, it is possible to configure and monitor the traffic of the ports. Only the packets from trusted source address can enter the organization"s network and the sources which are blacklisted and unauthorized address are denied access to the network. It is important to have firewalls to prevent the network from unauthorized access, but firewall does not guarantee this until and unless it is configured correctly. A firewall can be implemented using hardware as well as software or the combination of both.

Hardware Firewalls: example of hardware firewalls are routers through which the network is connected to the network outside the organization i.e., Internet.

Software Firewalls: These firewalls are installed on the server and client machines and it acts as a gateway to the organizations" network.

In the operating system like Windows 2003, Windows 2008 etc. it comes embedded with the operating system. The only thing a user need to do is to optimally configure the firewall according to their own requirement. The firewalls can be configured to follow "rules" and "policies" and based on these defined rules the firewalls can follow the following filtering mechanisms.

Proxy – all the outbound traffic is routed through proxies for monitoring and controlling the packet that are routed out of the organization.

Packet Filtering – based on the rules defined in the policies each packet is filtered by their type, port information, and source & destination information. The example of such characteristics is IP address, Domain names, port numbers, protocols etc. Basic packet filtering can be performed by routers.

Stateful Inspection: rather than going through all the field of a packet, key features are defined. The outgoing/incoming packets are judged based on those defined characteristics only.

The firewalls are an essential component of the organizations" network. They not only protect the organization against the virus and other malicious code but also prevent the hackers to use your network infrastructure to launch DOS attacks.

2.6 Steganography

It is a technique of hiding secret messages in a document file, image file, and program or protocol etc. such that the embedded message is invisible and can be retrieved using special software. Only the sender and the receiver know about the existence of the secret message in the image. The advantage of this technique is that these files are not easily suspected.

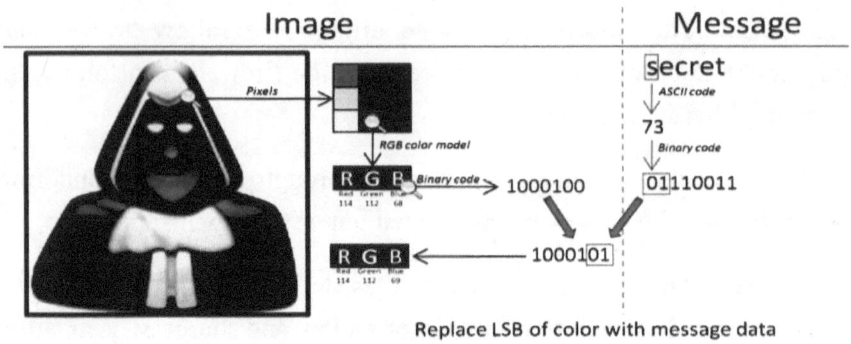

Figure 2.5: Steganography

There are many applications of steganography which includes sending secret messages without ringing the alarms, preventing secret files from unauthorized and accidental access and theft, digital watermarks for IPR issues, etc and it is shown in figure 2.5.

Let us discuss how the data is secretly embedded inside the cover file(the medium like image, video, audio, etc which is used to embed secret data) without being noticed. Let us take an example of an image file which is used as a cover medium. Each pixel of a high-resolution image is represented by 3 bytes (24 bits). If the 3 least significant bits of these 24 bits are altered and used for hiding the data, the resultant image, after embedded the data into it, will have unnoticeable change in the image quality and only a very experienced and trained eyes can detect this change. In this way, every pixel can be used to hide 3 bits of information.

Similarly, introducing a white noise in an audio file at regular or random interval can be used to hide data in an audio or video files. There are various free software's available for Steganography. Some of the popular ones are: QuickStego, Xiao, Tucows, OpenStego, etc.

Steganography in Streaming Media

Since the era of evolving network applications, steganography research has shifted from image steganography to steganography in streaming media such as Voice over Internet Protocol (VoIP).

In 2003, Giannoula et al. developed a data hiding technique leading to compressed forms of source video signals on a frame-by-frame basis.

In 2005, Dittmann et al. studied steganography and watermarking of multimedia contents such as VoIP.

In 2008, Yongfeng Huang and Shanyu Tang presented a novel approach to information hiding in low bit-rate VoIP speech stream, and their published work on steganography is the first-ever effort to improve the codebook partition by using Graph theory along with Quantization Index Modulation in low bit-rate streaming media.

In 2011 and 2012, Yongfeng Huang and Shanyu Tang devised new steganographic algorithms that use codec parameters as cover object to realise real-time covert VoIP steganography. Their findings were published in IEEE Transactions on Information Forensics and Security.

In 2024, Cheddad & Cheddad proposed a new framework for reconstructing lost or corrupted audio signals using a combination of machine learning techniques and latent information. The main idea of their paper is to enhance audio signal reconstruction by fusing steganography, halftoning (dithering), and state-of-the-art shallow and deep learning methods (e.g., RF, LSTM). This combination of steganography, halftoning, and machine learning for audio signal reconstruction may inspire further research in optimizing this approach or applying it to other domains, such as image reconstruction (i.e., inpainting).

Adaptive Steganography

Adaptive steganography is a technique for concealing information within digital media by tailoring the embedding process to the specific features of the cover medium. An example of this approach is demonstrated in the work. Their method develops a skin tone detection algorithm, capable of identifying facial features, which is then applied to adaptive steganography. By incorporating face rotation into their approach, the technique aims to enhance its adaptivity to conceal information in a manner that is both less detectable and more robust across various facial orientations within images. This strategy can potentially improve the efficacy of information hiding in both static images and video content.

Cyber-Physical Systems/Internet of Things

Academic work since 2012 demonstrated the feasibility of steganography for cyber-physical systems (CPS)/the Internet of Things (IoT). Some techniques of CPS/IoT steganography overlap with network steganography, i.e. hiding data in communication protocols used in CPS/ the IoT. However, specific techniques hide data in CPS components. For instance, data can be stored in unused registers of IoT/CPS components and in the states of IoT/CPS actuators.

Printed

Digital steganography output may be in the form of printed documents. A message, the plaintext, may be first encrypted by traditional means, producing a ciphertext. Then, an innocuous cover text is modified in some way so as to contain the ciphertext, resulting in the stegotext. For example, the letter size, spacing, typeface, or other characteristics of a cover text can be manipulated to carry the hidden message. Only a recipient who knows the technique used can recover the message and then decrypt it. Francis Bacon developed Bacon's cipher as such a technique.

The ciphertext produced by most digital steganography methods, however, is not printable. Traditional digital methods rely on perturbing noise in the channel file to hide the message, and as such, the channel file must be transmitted to the recipient with no additional noise from the transmission. Printing introduces much noise in the ciphertext, generally rendering the message unrecoverable. There are techniques that address this limitation, one notable example being ASCII Art Steganography.

Network

In 2015, a taxonomy of 109 network hiding methods was presented by Steffen Wendzel, Sebastian Zander et al. that summarized core concepts used in network steganography research. The taxonomy was developed further in recent years by several publications and authors and adjusted to new domains, such as CPS steganography.

In 1977, Kent concisely described the potential for covert channel signaling in general network communication protocols, even if the traffic is encrypted (in a footnote) in "Encryption-Based Protection for Interactive User/Computer Communication," Proceedings of the Fifth Data Communications Symposium, September 1977.

In 1987, Girling first studied covert channels on a local area network (LAN), identified and realised three obvious covert channels (two storage channels and one timing channel), and his research paper entitled "Covert channels in LAN's" published in IEEE Transactions on Software Engineering, vol. SE-13 of 2, in February 1987.

In 1989, Wolf implemented covert channels in LAN protocols, e.g. using the reserved fields, pad fields, and undefined fields in the TCP/IP protocol.

In 1997, Rowland used the IP identification field, the TCP initial sequence number and acknowledge sequence number fields in TCP/IP headers to build covert channels.

In 2002, Kamran Ahsan made an excellent summary of research on network steganography.

In 2005, Steven J. Murdoch and Stephen Lewis contributed a chapter entitled "Embedding Covert Channels into TCP/IP" in the "Information Hiding" book published by Springer.

All information hiding techniques that may be used to exchange steganograms in telecommunication networks can be classified under the general term of network steganography. This nomenclature was originally introduced by Krzysztof Szczypiorski in 2003. Contrary to typical steganographic methods that use digital media (images, audio and video files) to hide data, network steganography uses communication protocols' control elements and their intrinsic functionality. As a result, such methods can be harder to detect and eliminate.

Typical network steganography methods involve modification of the properties of a single network protocol. Such modification can be applied to the protocol data unit (PDU), to the time relations between the exchanged PDUs, or both (hybrid methods).

Moreover, it is feasible to utilize the relation between two or more different network protocols to enable secret communication. These applications fall under the term inter-protocol steganography. Alternatively, multiple network protocols can be used simultaneously to transfer hidden information and so-called control protocols can be embedded into steganographic communications to extend their capabilities, e.g. to allow dynamic overlay routing or the switching of utilized hiding methods and network protocols.

Network steganography covers a broad spectrum of techniques, which include, among others:

Steganophony – the concealment of messages in Voice-over-IP conversations, e.g. the employment of delayed or corrupted packets that would normally be ignored by the receiver (this method is called LACK – Lost Audio Packets Steganography), or, alternatively, hiding information in unused header fields.

WLAN Steganography – transmission of steganograms in Wireless Local Area Networks. A practical example of WLAN Steganography is the HICCUPS system (Hidden Communication System for Corrupted Networks)

Additional Terminology

Discussions of steganography generally use terminology analogous to and consistent with conventional radio and communications technology. However, some terms appear specifically in software and are easily confused. These are the most relevant ones to digital steganographic systems:

The payload is the data covertly communicated. The carrier is the signal, stream, or data file that hides the payload, which differs from the channel, which typically means the type of input, such as a JPEG image. The resulting signal, stream, or data file with the encoded payload is sometimes called the package, stego file, or covert message. The proportion of bytes, samples, or other signal elements modified to encode the payload is called the encoding density and is typically expressed as a number between 0 and 1.

In a set of files, the files that are considered likely to contain a payload are suspects. A suspect identified through some type of statistical analysis can be referred to as a candidate.

Countermeasures and Detection

Detecting physical steganography requires a careful physical examination, including the use of magnification, developer chemicals, and ultraviolet light. It is a time-consuming process with obvious resource implications, even in countries that employ many people to spy on other citizens. However, it is feasible to screen mail of certain suspected individuals or institutions, such as prisons or prisoner-of-war (POW) camps.

During World War II, prisoner of war camps gave prisoners specially-treated paper that would reveal invisible ink. An article in the 24 June 1948 issue of Paper Trade Journal by the Technical Director of the United States Government Printing Office had Morris S. Kantrowitz describe in general terms the development of this paper. Three prototype papers

(Sensicoat, Anilith, and Coatalith) were used to manufacture postcards and stationery provided to German prisoners of war in the US and Canada. If POWs tried to write a hidden message, the special paper rendered it visible. The US granted at least two patents related to the technology, one to Kantrowitz, U.S. patent 2,515,232, "Water-Detecting paper and Water-Detecting Coating Composition Therefor," patented 18 July 1950, and an earlier one, "Moisture-Sensitive Paper and the Manufacture Thereof," U.S. patent 2,445,586, patented 20 July 1948. A similar strategy issues prisoners with writing paper ruled with a water-soluble ink that runs in contact with water-based invisible ink.

In computing, steganographically encoded package detection is called steganalysis. The simplest method to detect modified files, however, is to compare them to known originals. For example, to detect information being moved through the graphics on a website, an analyst can maintain known clean copies of the materials and then compare them against the current contents of the site. The differences, if the carrier is the same, comprise the payload. In general, using extremely high compression rates makes steganography difficult but not impossible. Compression errors provide a hiding place for data, but high compression reduces the amount of data available to hold the payload, raising the encoding density, which facilitates easier detection (in extreme cases, even by casual observation).

There are a variety of basic tests that can be done to identify whether or not a secret message exists. This process is not concerned with the extraction of the message, which is a different process and a separate step. The most basic approaches of steganalysis are visual or aural attacks, structural attacks, and statistical attacks. These approaches attempt to detect the steganographic algorithms that were used. These algorithms range from unsophisticated to very sophisticated, with early algorithms being much easier to detect due to statistical anomalies that were present. The size of the message that is being hidden is a factor in how difficult it is to detect. The overall size of the cover object also plays a factor as well. If the cover object is small and the message is large, this can distort the statistics and make it easier to detect. A larger cover object with a small message decreases the statistics and gives it a better chance of going unnoticed.

Steganalysis that targets a particular algorithm has much better success as it is able to key in on the anomalies that are left behind. This is because the analysis can perform a targeted search to discover known tendencies since it is aware of the behaviors that it commonly exhibits. When analyzing an image the least significant bits of many images are actually not random. The camera sensor, especially lower-end sensors are not the best quality and can introduce some random bits. This can also be affected by the file compression done on the image. Secret messages can be introduced into the least significant bits in an image and then hidden. A steganography tool can be used to camouflage the secret message in the least significant bits but it can introduce a random area that is too perfect. This area of perfect randomization stands out and can be detected by comparing the least significant bits to the next-to-least significant bits on an image that hasn't been compressed.

Generally, though, there are many techniques known to be able to hide messages in data using steganographic techniques. None are, by definition, obvious when users employ standard applications, but some can be detected by specialist tools. Others, however, are resistant to detection—or rather it is not possible to reliably distinguish data containing a hidden message from data containing just noise—even when the most sophisticated analysis is performed. Steganography is being used to conceal and deliver more effective cyber-attacks, referred to as Stegware. The term Stegware was first introduced in 2017 to describe any malicious operation involving steganography as a vehicle to conceal an attack. Detection of steganography is challenging, and because of that, not an adequate defence. Therefore, the only way of defeating the threat is to transform data in a way that destroys any hidden messages, a process called Content Threat Removal.

Applications

Use in modern printersSome modern computer printers use steganography, including Hewlett-Packard and Xerox brand color laser printers. The printers add tiny yellow dots to each page. The barely-visible dots contain encoded printer serial numbers and date and time stamps.

Example From Modern Practice

The larger the cover message (in binary data, the number of bits) relative to the hidden message, the easier it is to hide the hidden message (as an analogy, the larger the "haystack", the easier it is to hide a "needle"). So digital pictures, which contain much data, are sometimes used to hide messages on the Internet and on other digital communication media. It is not clear how common this practice actually is.

For example, a 24-bit bitmap uses 8 bits to represent each of the three color values (red, green, and blue) of each pixel. The blue alone has 28 different levels of blue intensity. The difference between 111111112 and 111111102 in the value for blue intensity is likely to be undetectable by the human eye. Therefore, the least significant bit can be used more or less undetectably for something else other than color information. If that is repeated for the green and the red elements of each pixel as well, it is possible to encode one letter of ASCII text for every three pixels.

Stated somewhat more formally, the objective for making steganographic encoding difficult to detect is to ensure that the changes to the carrier (the original signal) because of the injection of the payload (the signal to covertly embed) are visually (and ideally, statistically) negligible. The changes are indistinguishable from the noise floor of the carrier. All media can be a carrier, but media with a large amount of redundant or compressible information is better suited.

From an information theoretical point of view, that means that the channel must have more capacity than the "surface" signal requires. There must be redundancy. For a digital image, it may be noise from the imaging element; for digital audio, it may be noise from recording techniques or amplification equipment. In general, electronics that digitize an analog signal suffer from several noise sources, such as thermal noise, flicker noise, and shot noise. The noise provides enough variation in the captured digital information that it can be exploited as a noise cover for hidden data. In addition, lossy compression schemes (such as JPEG) always introduce some error to the decompressed data, and it is possible to exploit that for steganographic use, as well.

Although steganography and digital watermarking seem similar, they are not. In steganography, the hidden message should remain intact until it reaches its destination. Steganography can be used for digital watermarking in which a message (being simply an identifier) is hidden in an image so that its source can be tracked or verified (for example, Coded Anti-Piracy) or even just to identify an image (as in the EURion constellation). In such a case, the technique of hiding the message (here, the watermark) must be robust to prevent tampering. However, digital watermarking sometimes requires a brittle watermark, which can be modified easily, to check whether the image has been tampered with. That is the key difference between steganography and digital watermarking.

Alleged Use By Intelligence Services

In 2010, the Federal Bureau of Investigation alleged that the Russian foreign intelligence service uses customized steganography software for embedding encrypted text messages inside image files for certain communications with "illegal agents" (agents without diplomatic cover) stationed abroad.

On 23 April 2019 the U.S. Department of Justice unsealed an indictment charging Xiaoqing Zheng, a Chinese businessman and former Principal Engineer at General Electric, with 14 counts of conspiring to steal intellectual property and trade secrets from General Electric. Zheng had allegedly used steganography to exfiltrate 20,000 documents from

General Electric to Tianyi Aviation Technology Co. in Nanjing, China, a company the FBI accused him of starting with backing from the Chinese government.

Distributed Steganography

There are distributed steganography methods, including methodologies that distribute the payload through multiple carrier files in diverse locations to make detection more difficult. For example, U.S. patent 8,527,779 by cryptographer William Easttom (Chuck Easttom).

Online Challenge

The puzzles that are presented by Cicada 3301 incorporate steganography with cryptography and other solving techniques since 2012. Puzzles involving steganography have also been featured in other alternative reality games.

The communications of The May Day mystery incorporate steganography and other solving techniques since 1981.

Computer Malware

It is possible to steganographically hide computer malware into digital images, videos, audio and various other files in order to evade detection by antivirus software. This type of malware is called stegomalware. It can be activated by external code, which can be malicious or even non-malicious if some vulnerability in the software reading the file is exploited.

Stegomalware can be removed from certain files without knowing whether they contain stegomalware or not. This is done through content disarm and reconstruction (CDR) software, and it involves reprocessing the entire file or removing parts from it. Actually, detecting stegomalware in a file can be difficult and may involve testing the file behavior in virtual environments or deep learning analysis of the file.

Steganalysis

Stegoanalytical Algorithms

Stegoanalytical algorithms can be cataloged in different ways, highlighting: according to the available information and according to the purpose sought.

According to the Information Available

There is the possibility of cataloging these algorithms based on the information held by the stegoanalyst in terms of clear and encrypted messages. It is a technique similar to cryptography, however, they have several differences:

Chosen stego attack: the stegoanalyst perceives the final target stego and the steganographic algorithm used.

Known cover attack: the stegoanalyst comprises the initial conductive target and the final target stego.

Known stego attack: the stegoanalyst knows the initial carrier target and the final target stego, in addition to the algorithm used.

Stego only attack: the stegoanalyst perceives exclusively the stego target.

Chosen message attack: the stegoanalyst, following a message selected by him, originates a stego target.

Known message attack: the stegoanalyst owns the stego target and the hidden message, which is known to them.

According to the Purpose Sought

The principal purpose of steganography is to transfer information unnoticed, however, it is possible for an attacker to have two different pretensions:

Passive steganalysis: does not alter the target stego, therefore, it examines the target stego in order to establish whether it carries hidden information and recovers the hidden message, the key used or both.

Active steganalysis: changes the initial stego target, therefore, it seeks to suppress the transfer of information, if it exists.

Chapter 3

Cybersecurity Initiatives in India

3.1 Introduction

Policy Frameworks

Policy frameworks like the National Cyber Security Policy and guidelines under the Information Technology Act provide a structured approach to cybersecurity, addressing the diverse needs of sectors ranging from finance to infrastructure. They establish clear standards for data protection, cyber resilience, and risk management, ensuring a cohesive national strategy. Furthermore, these frameworks encourage collaboration between public and private sectors, fostering an ecosystem of shared knowledge and resources.

By continually updating regulations to keep pace with emerging threats and technological advancements, regulatory bodies and policy frameworks in India ensure a proactive stance against cyber risks, thereby fortifying the country's digital sovereignty and economic stability.

Policy Frameworks

India has made substantial progress in developing its cybersecurity framework. Key initiatives include the establishment of the Indian Computer Emergency Response Team (CERT-In), the National Cyber Security Policy 2013, and various sector-specific guidelines. Despite these efforts, the country continues to face numerous cybersecurity challenges.

National Cybersecurity Policy, 2013

The National Cybersecurity Policy of 2013 is a comprehensive framework established by the Government of India aimed at protecting the country's information infrastructure and managing the associated risks. This policy was introduced in response to the increasing threat landscape and the need for a robust cybersecurity strategy to safeguard critical information infrastructure.

3.2 Objectives of the Policy

1. To create a secure Cyber Ecosystem: The policy emphasizes the creation of a secure and resilient cyber ecosystem within the country. This involves establishing necessary regulatory frameworks, enabling legal, technical, and operational measures to address cyber threats.
2. Enhancing capacities: A key goal is to enhance the capabilities of various stakeholders including government entities, businesses, and individuals to effectively respond to and mitigate cyber threats. This includes training and awareness programs aimed at improving the cybersecurity posture.
3. Strengthening regulatory frameworks: The policy aims to strengthen existing legal frameworks to address the issues of cybercrime more effectively. This includes updating laws, improving enforcement mechanisms, and ensuring international cooperation.
4. Promoting research and development: Encouraging R&D in cybersecurity technologies is a significant component of the policy. This involves supporting innovation and the development of new technologies to counter evolving cyber threats.
5. Protection of Critical Information Infrastructure (CII): The policy prioritizes the protection of CIIs such as banking, telecommunications, defence, energy, and other vital sectors. It aims to develop a robust framework for identifying, assessing, and mitigating risks to these infrastructures.

3.3 Key Components

Institutional Structures: The policy calls for the establishment of various bodies and institutions to oversee and implement cybersecurity measures. This includes the National Critical Information Infrastructure Protection Centre (NCIIPC) responsible for securing critical information infrastructure.

Cybersecurity Assurance Framework: It includes the development of frameworks to ensure that all entities handling critical data comply with prescribed cybersecurity standards and best practices.

Public-Private Partnerships: Recognizing the role of private sector entities in managing and operating critical infrastructure, the policy promotes collaboration between public and private sectors for effective cybersecurity management.

Information Sharing and Cooperation: The policy encourages the creation of mechanisms for sharing threat intelligence and information on vulnerabilities among various stakeholders, both nationally and internationally.

Capacity Building and Skill Development: It stresses the need for enhancing the skills of professionals working in the field of cybersecurity through specialized training programs and certifications.

3.4 Challenges and Implementation

While the National Cybersecurity Policy, 2013, sets a robust foundation for securing India's cyberspace, its implementation has faced several challenges. These include

Coordination among stakeholders: Ensuring effective coordination among various government agencies, private sector entities, and international partners remains a complex task.

Resource constraints: Allocating sufficient resources, both financial and human, to implement various measures outlined in the policy has been challenging.

Rapid technological advancements: Keeping up with the fast-paced evolution of cyber threats and technologies requires continuous updates to the policy and associated frameworks.

Awareness and training: Ensuring widespread awareness and training across all levels of society, from government officials to the general public, is an ongoing effort.

The National Cybersecurity Policy, 2013, marks a significant step towards building a secure and resilient cyberspace in India. It lays down a comprehensive strategy for addressing the multifaceted challenges of cybersecurity. While the policy provides a strong foundation, continuous efforts in terms of coordination, resource allocation, and adaptation to emerging threats are essential for its successful implementation and for safeguarding India's critical information infrastructure.

Information Technology Act, 2000

The Information Technology Act, 2000, is a landmark legislation in India that provides a legal framework for electronic governance and addresses issues related to cybercrime and electronic commerce. Enacted on October 17, 2000, this act represents a crucial step towards adapting the country's legal framework to the digital age, ensuring that electronic transactions are legally recognized and protected.

3.4.1 Objectives of the IT Act

Legal recognition of electronic transactions: One of the primary objectives of the IT Act, 2000, is to provide legal recognition to electronic records and digital signatures, thereby facilitating electronic commerce and transactions.

Prevention of cybercrime: The Act addresses various types of cybercrimes, including hacking, identity theft, and digital fraud, laying down penalties and punishments for offenders.

Promoting E-Governance: The IT Act promotes the use of electronic records and digital signatures in government operations and services, enhancing efficiency and transparency.

4Facilitating E-Commerce: By recognizing electronic contracts and transactions, the Act aims to boost the growth of e-commerce, providing a secure and reliable environment for digital business activities.

Key Provisions of the IT Act

Legal recognition of electronic records: Sections 4 and 5 of the Act grant legal recognition to electronic records and digital signatures, enabling their use in legal contracts, agreements, and other formal documents.

Digital signatures: The Act defines digital signatures and outlines the process for their authentication, making them equivalent to handwritten signatures in electronic transactions.

Regulation of Certifying Authorities: The Act establishes a framework for the regulation of certifying authorities, which are responsible for issuing digital certificates and ensuring the security of digital signatures.

Cybercrimes and penalties: Chapter XI of the Act specifies various cybercrimes and prescribes penalties and punishments for offenses such as hacking, unauthorized access, identity theft, and cyber terrorism.

Adjudication of disputes: The Act provides for the appointment of adjudicating officers to handle disputes related to electronic transactions and cybercrimes, ensuring a streamlined process for resolution.

Establishment of the Cyber Appellate Tribunal: The Act establishes the Cyber Appellate Tribunal to hear appeals against the orders of adjudicating officers, providing a higher level of judicial oversight.

Offenses by Intermediaries: The Act outlines the liability of intermediaries, such as internet service providers and web hosting services, for third-party content. It provides them with a safe harbour if they follow due diligence and take necessary actions upon receiving complaints.

Amendments and Updates

The IT Act, 2000, has undergone several amendments to address the evolving nature of cyber threats and technological advancements. The most significant amendment came in 2008, which introduced several new provisions, including:

Cyber Terrorism: The Act now includes provisions to address cyber terrorism, defining it and prescribing severe penalties for those involved in cyber terrorism activities.

Obscenity and Pornography: The amendment expanded the scope of the Act to include offenses related to the publication and transmission of obscene material, including child pornography.

Challenges

Despite its comprehensive nature, the IT Act, 2000, has faced several challenges and criticisms:

Ambiguity and interpretation: Some provisions of the Act have been criticized for being vague and open to interpretation, leading to potential misuse and arbitrary enforcement.

Implementation and enforcement: Effective implementation and enforcement of the Act's provisions remain a challenge due to a lack of awareness, inadequate resources, and technical expertise among law enforcement agencies.

The Information Technology Act, 2000, serves as a foundational legal framework for governing electronic transactions and combating cybercrime in India. It has played a pivotal role in fostering the growth of e-commerce, promoting e-governance, and enhancing cybersecurity.

However, continuous efforts to update and refine the Act are essential to address emerging cyber threats and technological advancements, ensuring that it remains relevant and effective in the digital age.

National Cybersecurity Strategy, 2020

The National Cybersecurity Strategy, 2020, represents a significant step forward in India's efforts to secure its cyberspace against evolving threats. This strategy, developed by the National Security Council Secretariat (NSCS), aims to create a safe, secure, and resilient cyberspace for citizens, businesses, and the government.

Objectives of the Strategy

Secure National Cyberspace: The primary goal is to secure India's cyberspace from cyber threats by enhancing the protection of critical information infrastructure and creating a robust cybersecurity framework.

Strengthen institutions and capacities: The strategy aims to build and strengthen institutions and capacities across sectors to respond effectively to cybersecurity incidents.

Promote cyber awareness and skills: Enhancing cyber awareness among citizens and promoting the development of skills and competencies in cybersecurity is a key focus.

Foster international cooperation: The strategy emphasizes the importance of international cooperation in tackling cyber threats and establishing norms for responsible state behavior in cyberspace.

Key Pillars of the Strategy

Critical Information Infrastructure (CII) protection: The strategy outlines measures to identify and protect CII sectors such as banking, telecommunications, energy, and defence. This includes regular risk assessments, vulnerability management, and the establishment of robust incident response mechanisms.

Institutional framework and governance: Strengthening the existing institutional framework, including the role of agencies like the Indian Computer Emergency Response Team (CERT-In) and the National Critical Information Infrastructure Protection Centre (NCIIPC), to ensure a coordinated response to cyber incidents.

Capacity building and skill development: Developing a skilled cybersecurity workforce through education, training, and certification programs. This includes integrating cybersecurity education into school and university curricula and promoting research and development in cybersecurity technologies.

Cybercrime prevention and law enforcement: Enhancing the capabilities of law enforcement agencies to prevent, detect, investigate, and prosecute cybercrimes. This involves updating legal frameworks, improving digital forensics capabilities, and fostering cooperation with international law enforcement agencies.

Public-Private partnership: Encouraging collaboration between government and private sector entities to share information on threats and vulnerabilities and to develop joint strategies for protecting cyberspace.

Cyber hygiene and awareness: Promoting cyber hygiene practices among individuals and organizations to prevent cyber incidents. This includes public awareness campaigns, workshops, and the dissemination of best practices for cybersecurity.

International engagement: Engaging with international partners to share best practices, participate in global cybersecurity initiatives, and contribute to the development of international norms and standards for cybersecurity.

3.5 Strategic Actions and Initiatives

National Cybersecurity Coordination Centre (NCCC): Operationalizing the NCCC to provide real-time situational awareness and coordinate responses to cybersecurity incidents.

Cybersecurity training and certification: Establishing national-level programs for cybersecurity training and certification to ensure a steady pipeline of skilled professionals.

Sectoral CERTs: Creating sector-specific Computer Emergency Response Teams (CERTs) to address unique cybersecurity challenges in different sectors.

Research and innovation: Promoting research and innovation in cybersecurity through funding, grants, and partnerships with academic institutions and industry.

Legislative measures: Reviewing and updating existing cybersecurity laws and regulations to address emerging threats and challenges. This includes developing a robust data protection framework.

Challenges and Implementation

The implementation of the National Cybersecurity Strategy, 2020, faces several challenges

Coordination and collaboration: Ensuring effective coordination among various stakeholders, including government agencies, private sector entities, and international partners.

Resource allocation: Allocating adequate resources, both financial and human, to implement the strategy's initiatives effectively.

Rapid technological changes: Keeping pace with the fast-evolving cyber threat landscape and technological advancements.

Awareness and education: Promoting widespread awareness and understanding of cybersecurity among the general public and organizations.

The National Cybersecurity Strategy, 2020, is a comprehensive framework aimed at securing India's digital infrastructure and ensuring a resilient cyberspace. By focusing on critical information infrastructure protection, capacity building, public – private partnerships, and international cooperation, the strategy aims to create a robust cybersecurity ecosystem. Successful implementation of this strategy is essential to protect national interests, promote economic growth, and safeguard the digital lives of Indian citizens in an increasingly interconnected world.

Initiatives Taken by Indian Government for Cyber Security

Maintaining adequate cyber security measures in today's high tech digital environment is crucial and the best way to safeguard the IT infrastructure of the organizations. Not only are these threats harming the businesses, but also government authorities. Initiating cyber security measures by the government of India will help maintain a cyber-secure environment and mitigate the risks associated with the threat. The number of cyber security incidents has increased over the years. Mr PP Choudhary, minister of state for electronics and IT stated that 44679, 49455, 50362 cyber security incidents took place in India during the years 2014, 2015 and 2016, as stated by the information collected by India's computer emergency response team (CERT-in). Although the government has taken certain cyber security initiatives as discussed below, more aggressive measures are required to meet the challenge.

3.6 Initiatives Taken by The Indian Government on Cyber Security

1. The Indian Computer Emergency Response Team (CERT-In)

The advancement in the Indian Computer Emergency Response Team (CERT-In), which operates as the national agency to address the country's cyber security, has helped reduce the rate of cyber attacks on government networks

2. Cyber Surakshit Bharat

Aiming to strengthen the cybersecurity ecosystem in India and following the Government's vision of a "digital India," the Ministry of Electronics and Information Technology (MeitY) has launched the Cyber Surakshit Bharat initiative

The program was in partnership with the National Electronic Governance Division (NeGD).

National Critical Information Infrastructure Protection Center (NCIIPC).

NCIIPC is a central government establishment, formed to protect critical information about our country, which has an enormous impact on national security, economic growth, and public health care

NCIIPC has mainly identified the following as "critical sectors"-

- Power & Energy
- Banking, Financial Services & Insurance
- Telecom Transport
- Government
- Strategic & Public Enterprises

3. Appointment of Chief Information Security Officers

The Indian Government has published a written guideline for CISOs of government organizations, outlining best practices for safeguarding apps, infrastructure, and compliance

Chief Information Security Officers (CISOs) can identify and document the security requirements that may arise with each technical innovation

4. Personal Data Protection Bill

The most important one for Indian citizens is the approval of the Personal Data Protection Bill by the Union Government to protect Indian users from global breaches, which focuses on data localization

The bill involves the storage and processing of any critical information related to people only in India

It strictly states that individuals' sensitive personal data is to be stored locally; however, it can be processed abroad under certain conditions

The bill also aims to make social media companies more accountable and push them to solve the spread of offensive content

5. Cyber Swachhta Kendra (Botnet Cleaning and Malware Analysis Center)

The "Digital Swachhta Kendra" (Botnet Cleaning and Malware Analysis Center) is a part of the Government of India's Digital India drive, overseen by the Ministry of Electronics and Information Technology (MeitY), determined to make secure cyberspace all through India by distinguishing botnet contaminations and advising, empowering cleaning, and end-client security systems to forestall new diseases

The "Cyber Swachhta Kendra" (Botnet Cleaning and Malware Analysis Center) is intended to address the goals of the "National Cybersecurity Policy," which calls for the development of a secure cybernetic ecosystem in the country

The centre works in close coordination and collaboration with Internet service providers and antivirus/product companies

The website provides users with information and tools to help them protect their systems/devices. Following Section 70B of the Information Technology Act 2000, this centre is run by the Indian Computer Emergency Response Team (CERT-In)

6. National Cyber Security Policy, 2013

The Policy's goal is to create safe and resilient cyberspace for citizens, businesses, and the Government

The mission is to provide protection to cyberspace information and infrastructure, develop capabilities to prevent and respond to cyberattacks, and minimize damage through coordinated efforts of institutional structures, people, processes, and technology

To create a workforce of 500,000 trained cybersecurity professionals in the next 5 years through capacity building, skills development and training

Through appropriate legislative intervention, enable effective cybercrime prevention, investigation, and prosecution, as well as the enhancement of law enforcement capabilities

3.7 Safeguarding India's Digital Landscape

India has emerged as a global leader in the digital landscape, with a staggering 936 million Internet subscribers (Till Dec 2023, TRAI), transforming it into one of the largest connected nations worldwide. Termed as 'Digital Nagriks', Indians are increasingly integrating the internet into their daily lives, relying on it for essential needs such as business transactions, education, financial activities, and accessing government services digitally.

Recognizing the critical importance of a secure digital environment, the Government of India has been implementing robust policies aimed at safeguarding its vast online community. These measures are designed to ensure a safe, trusted, and secure cyberspace amidst the growing prevalence of cyber threats and attacks in today's interconnected world and these are shown in figure 3.1.

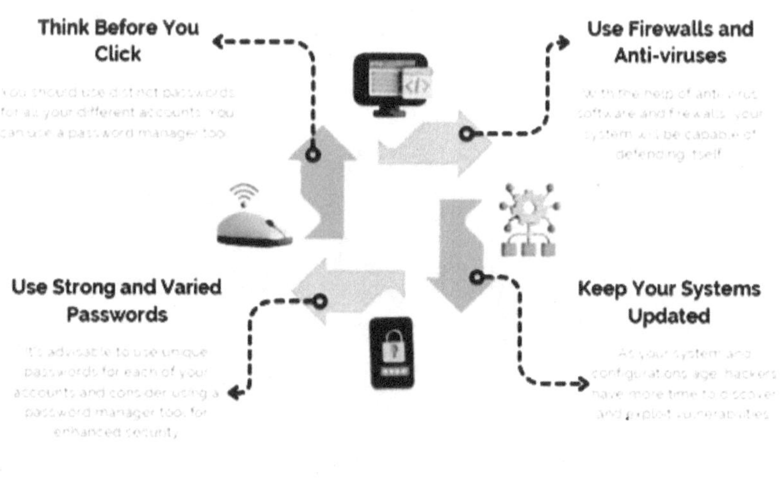

Figure 3.1: Prevalence of cyber threats and attacks

Understanding CERT-In

Established as the national agency for incident response under Section 70B of the Information Technology Act, 2000, the Indian Computer Emergency Response Team (CERT-In) plays an imperative role in safeguarding India's cyber landscape. Operating a 24x7 incident response Help Desk, CERT-In ensures timely responses to reported cybersecurity incidents. The organization offers comprehensive Incident Prevention and Response services alongside Security Quality Management Services to enhance cybersecurity measures across the nation.

The Indian Computer Emergency Response Team (CERT-In) has registered several cases of cybercrimes during the last three years. The details are as follows.

Year	Phishing incidents	Network scanning and probing	Virus/Malware incidents	Website hacking incidents	Cyber Security incidents
2021	215	86585	9203	18	122764
2022	1145	10220	2559	57	27482
2023	401	12330	1185	39	23158

The data was provided by Minister of State Electronics & Information Technology (MoS) Jitin Prasada on 24 July 2024 in Lok Sabha.

3.8 CERT-In's Efforts to Combat cybercrime

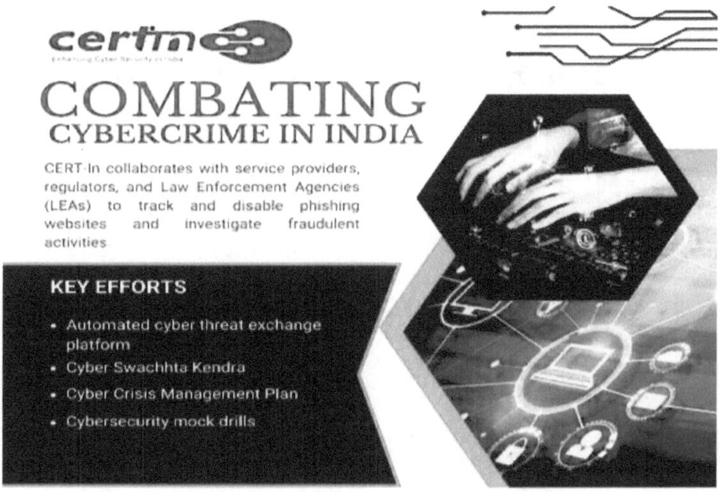

Figure 3.2: CERT-In's efforts to combat cybercrime

CERT-In shown in figure 3.2 collaborates with service providers, regulators, and Law Enforcement Agencies (LEAs) to track and disable phishing websites and investigate fraudulent activities.

CERT-In issues advisory to Ministries outlining measures to strengthen cyber security for entities handling digital personal data, including sensitive information.

CERT-In issues advisories through RBI for audits and implementation of security practices by entities issuing prepaid payment instruments.

CERT-In operates an automated cyber threat exchange platform for sharing tailored alerts across sectors.

CERT-In manages the Cyber Swachhta Kendra for detecting and removing malicious programs, providing cyber security tips.

The platform has formulated a Cyber Crisis Management Plan for countering cyber-attacks across government and critical sectors.

CERT-In conducts cybersecurity mock drills to assess readiness of organizations; 92 drills conducted with participation from diverse sectors.

CERT-In conducts training and workshops on specialized cyber security topics and offers a self-paced Cyber Security Foundation Course in collaboration with National Institute of Securities Markets and C-DAC.

3.9 Government Initiatives to Enhance Cybersecurity Awareness

Cyber Crime Coordination Centre

Figure 3.3: Cyber Crime Coordination Centre

The Indian Government of figure 3.3 has established the Indian Cyber Crime Coordination Centre (14C) to enhance the coordinated response of law enforcement agencies (LEAs) to cybercrimes. This initiative aims to provide a cohesive framework for addressing digital threats comprehensively. Concurrently, the National Cyber Crime Reporting Portal (https://cybercrime.gov.in) has been launched, enabling the public to report cybercrimes directly. Notably, incidents reported through this portal are automatically routed to the respective State/UT law enforcement agencies for prompt and efficient handling by legal provisions. These efforts underscore the government's commitment to bolstering cyber security and empowering citizens to contribute actively to cybercrime prevention.

Citizen Financial Cyber Fraud Reporting and Management System

The Government launched the 'Citizen Financial Cyber Fraud Reporting and Management System' to facilitate the immediate reporting of financial frauds and prevent fund siphoning by fraudsters. A toll-free helpline number, '1930', has been operationalized to assist with lodging online cyber complaints, ensuring swift response and support for victims of cyber fraud.

Multifaceted Awareness Campaigns

The Central Government has implemented a multifaceted approach to enhance the response to cybercrimes comprehensively. This includes extensive awareness campaigns aimed at educating the public and stakeholders about cyber threats, issuing regular alerts and advisories to highlight emerging risks, conducting specialized capacity-building and training programs for law enforcement personnel, prosecutors, and judicial officers, and improving cyber forensic facilities to bolster investigative capabilities. These initiatives collectively strengthen the government's framework for addressing cybercrimes in a coordinated manner across the country.

3.10 Digital Personal Data Protection Act: Protecting Citizen Rights

The Digital Personal Data Protection Act, 2023 upholds individuals' rights to safeguard their personal data, incorporating established principles for data protection. These principles include obtaining consent for lawful and transparent use of personal data, limiting its use to specified purposes, minimizing data collection to necessary levels, ensuring data accuracy and timely updates, restricting storage duration to the required period, implementing robust security measures, and enforcing accountability through penalties for breaches and data adjudication.

Additionally, the Act imposes stringent protections on personal data transfers, as exemplified by the Reserve Bank of India's directive under

Section 10(2) and Section 18 of the Payment and Settlement Systems Act, 2007, mandating the storage of payment system data within India. These provisions underscore the Act's commitment to robust data protection standards and restrictions on personal data transfers, which remain in effect under its framework.

3.11 Strengthening India's Cyber Defence

The year 2024 has ushered in a new era of digital threats, with Artificial Intelligence (AI) and its various manifestations, including Generative AI and Artificial General Intelligence (AGI), at the forefront of security concerns. The potential for digital attacks, disinformation campaigns, and cyber threats remains high. The recent global disruption caused by a Microsoft Windows software update glitch serves as a stark reminder of the vulnerabilities in our interconnected digital infrastructure.

For India, as with the rest of the world, the threat landscape is evolving rapidly. From AI-enabled deep fakes to sophisticated cyber-attacks targeting critical infrastructure, the challenges are multifaceted and growing in complexity. The rise in cyber fraud affecting ordinary citizens, including phishing attempts, identity theft, and financial scams, underscores the need for heightened awareness and robust cybersecurity measures. As we navigate this new digital reality, it is imperative for both the public and private sectors in India to prioritize cybersecurity, invest in advanced protective measures, and foster a culture of digital vigilance to safeguard national security and individual privacy.

What are the Current Major Cyber Threats that India is Facing?

The Ransomware Rampage: India witnessed an increase in ransomware attacks recently with the healthcare sector being particularly vulnerable.

Security software maker Quick Heal stated it has detected over 48000 instances of the WannaCry ransomware attack in India.

The attack on the All-India Institute of Medical Sciences (AIIMS) Delhi in November 2022.

There were at least 6,000 attempts to hack the server of the Indian Council of Medical Research (ICMR).

Phishing Paradox: India recorded over 79 million phishing attacks in 2023. The finance sector bore the brunt, accounting for the majority of all phishing attacks.

Examples include the Phishing Campaigns targeting State Bank of India users, where fraudsters sent fake SMS messages to millions of customers, attempting to steal their banking credentials.

This trend underscores the importance of user education and advanced email security solutions.

The Cloud Conundrum: As India rapidly adopts cloud technologies, with the overall Indian Public Cloud Services (PCS) market expected to reach USD 23.2 billion by 2028, cloud security threats have become a major concern.

In 2023, a significant data breach at Air India exposed the personal data of 3.5 million passengers, attributed to a compromise in its cloud service provider's systems.

This incident highlights the need for robust cloud security strategies, including proper configuration, access management, and continuous monitoring.

The IoT Invasion: With India's IoT market projected to reach USD 9.28 billion by 2025, the security of Internet of Things (IoT) devices has become a critical issue.

Researchers discovered a vulnerability in millions of smart meters deployed across India, potentially allowing hackers to manipulate power consumption data.

This discovery emphasizes the need for stringent security standards and regular updates for IoT devices in both consumer and industrial settings.

The Supply Chain Siege: India's digital supply chains faced unprecedented attacks in 2023, with a rampant increase in software supply chain vulnerabilities.

The SolarWinds-like attack on the IT services giant in 2023 is a prominent example.

This incident exposed the cascading effect of supply chain attacks and highlighted the need for rigorous vendor risk management and software integrity verification processes across Indian industries.

The Crypto Crimes Wave: According to a report published by 'Broadband India Forum' Cryptocurrency theft grew with roughly $3.2 billion worth stolen in 2021, a 516% increase compared to 2020.

The infamous WazirX Crypto Heist which compromised 45% of WazirX's crypto assets, has highlighted significant vulnerabilities highlighted the vulnerabilities in digital asset platforms.

This trend calls for stronger regulations, enhanced cybersecurity measures for crypto exchanges, and increased user awareness about safe crypto practices.

The Deepfake Dilemma: India witnessed a 230% increase in deepfake videos in 2023, with political misinformation campaigns leading the charge.

The viral deep fake video of a prominent Indian politician making inflammatory statements during the 2024 election campaign caused significant social unrest.

This incident highlights the urgent need for deepfake detection technologies, stricter content moderation policies, and public awareness campaigns about digital media literacy.

Lack of Cybersecurity Professionals: India faces a severe shortage of skilled cybersecurity professionals, leaving organizations vulnerable to cyber threats.

India has a shortage of 8 lakh cybersecurity professionals. This shortage is particularly acute in emerging technologies like AI and cloud security.

The lack of expertise hampers the implementation of robust cybersecurity measures and incident response capabilities, making it a critical threat to India's overall cybersecurity posture.

The Honey Trap Hazard: Honey trapping has emerged as a significant cyber threat in India, particularly targeting government officials, military personnel, and high-profile individuals.

This method involves creating fake social media profiles, usually of attractive individuals, to lure targets into compromising situations or divulging sensitive information.

In 2023, the Indian Army reported a dramatic increase in honey trapping attempts on its personnel compared to the previous year.

Another DRDO senior technical officer was detained in 2023 on suspicion of giving information about India's missile testing to a Pakistani intelligence operative.

What are the Key Government Initiatives Related to Cybersecurity in India?

National Cyber Security Policy: The policy outlines objectives and strategies to protect cyberspace information and infrastructure, develop capabilities to prevent and respond to cyber-attacks, and minimize damages through coordinated efforts across institutional structures, people, processes, and technology.

Indian Cyber Crime Coordination Centre (I4C): To provide a comprehensive and coordinated framework for law enforcement agencies to tackle cyber crimes.

Components

- National Cyber Crime Threat Analytics Unit
- National Cyber Crime Reporting Portal
- National Cyber Crime Training Centre
- Cyber Crime Ecosystem Management Unit
- National Cyber Crime Research and Innovation Centre
- National Cyber Crime Forensic Laboratory Ecosystem

Platform for Joint Cyber Crime Investigation Team

Computer Emergency Response Team – India (CERT-In): An organization under the Ministry of Electronics and Information Technology (MeitY) responsible for collecting, analyzing, and disseminating information on cyber incidents, as well as issuing alerts on cybersecurity threats.

Cyber Surakshit Bharat Initiative: To raise awareness about cyber crimes and implement safety measures for Chief Information Security Officers (CISOs) and frontline IT staff across all government departments.

Cyber Swachhta Kendra (Botnet Cleaning and Malware Analysis Centre): Launched in 2017, this center aims to create a secure cyberspace by detecting botnet infections in India and notifying users to enable the cleaning and securing of their systems to prevent further infections.

National Critical Information Infrastructure Protection Centre (NCIIPC): Established to protect Critical Information Infrastructure (CII) in sectors such as power, banking, telecom, transport, government, and strategic enterprises.

CII is defined as a computer resource whose destruction would have a debilitating impact on national security, economy, public health, or safety.

Defence Cyber Agency (DCyA)A tri-service command of the Indian Armed Forces responsible for handling cybersecurity threats.

The DCyA has the capability to conduct cyber operations, including hacking, surveillance, data recovery, encryption, and countermeasures against various cyber threat actors.

Digital Personal Data Protection Act 2023: This landmark legislation aims to protect the digital personal data of individuals in India and regulate the collection, storage, processing, and sharing of such data.

Key Features

- Establishes a Data Protection Board of India to enforce compliance
- Requires explicit consent for data collection and processing
- Mandates data fiduciaries to implement reasonable security safeguards

What Measures Can India Adopt to Bolster its Cybersecurity?

Cyber Fusion Centers: Establish regional Cyber Fusion Centers to facilitate real-time threat intelligence sharing between public and private sectors.

Implement advanced AI and machine learning systems for predictive threat analysis.

Create a centralized incident response team capable of rapid deployment to address major cyber incidents.

Conduct regular joint cyber exercises involving multiple stakeholders to test and improve coordination.

Digital Literacy Crusade: Launch a nationwide digital literacy campaign targeting all demographics, with a focus on cybersecurity awareness.

Integrate cybersecurity education into school curricula from secondary to higher education levels.

Develop a mobile app providing real-time cybersecurity tips and threat alerts to citizens.

Conduct regular cyber hygiene workshops in rural areas using local languages and relatable scenarios.

Partner with popular social media influencers to spread cybersecurity awareness among youth.

Strengthening Current Data Protection Framework: India should strengthen the existing Digital Personal Data Protection Act 2023 by incorporating provisions for regulating AI powered breaches of personal data, imposing stricter penalties for breaches, and enforcing rigorous implementation and scrutiny.

Enhancing the current act will address emerging threats without duplicating legislative efforts.

Secure-by-Design Initiative: Promote a 'Secure-by-Design' approach in software and hardware development across industries.

Establish a national cybersecurity product certification program to ensure adherence to security standards.

Offer grants and funding for startups focusing on developing innovative cybersecurity solutions.

Create a dedicated R&D fund for quantum-resistant cryptography to prepare for future threats.

AI-Powered Cyber Defense: Invest in developing AI-powered cybersecurity solutions tailored to India's unique threat landscape.

Implement machine learning algorithms for anomaly detection in network traffic and user behavior.

Develop AI-driven threat hunting capabilities to proactively identify and neutralize emerging cyber threats.

Supply Chain Fortification: Implement a comprehensive supply chain risk management framework for both hardware and software procurement.

Conduct regular security assessments of third-party vendors and service providers.

Develop a national database of trusted suppliers and mandate its use in government and critical sector procurements.

Implement blockchain technology for enhanced traceability and integrity in digital supply chains.

Cloud Citadel-Securing India's Digital Sky: Establish a national cloud security framework with stringent compliance requirements for all cloud service providers.

Implement mandatory encryption for all data stored in the cloud, addressing vulnerabilities like those in the Air India breach.

Create a Cloud Security Operations Center to monitor and respond to threats across public cloud services.

Deepfake Defense: Implement strict content verification protocols for all major social media platforms operating in India.

Create a rapid response team to address viral deepfakes during critical periods like elections.

Launch a public awareness campaign on identifying and reporting deepfakes.

The Cyber Warrior Initiative: India should launch a comprehensive "Cyber Warrior Initiative" to address the critical shortage of cybersecurity professionals.

This program would involve partnering with universities to develop specialized cybersecurity curricula, establishing a national cybersecurity scholarship program, and creating a cyber reserve force.

Implementing a national certification program and offering tax incentives to companies investing in employee cybersecurity training would further strengthen the workforce.

Chapter 4

Security for Cloud and IoT Environments

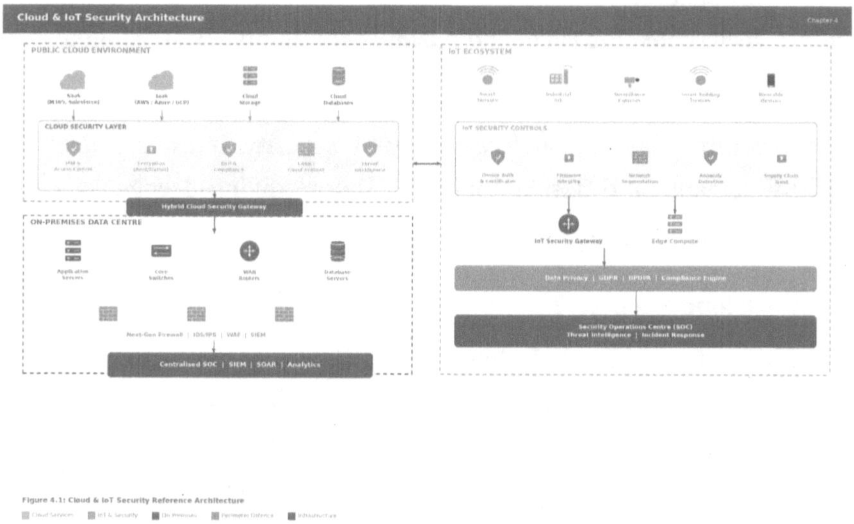

Figure 4.1: Cloud & IoT Security Reference Architecture

4.1 Cloud Security Definition

Cloud security is a discipline of cyber security dedicated to securing cloud computing systems. This includes keeping data private and safe across online-based infrastructure, applications, and platforms. Securing these systems involves the efforts of cloud providers and the clients that use them, whether an individual, small to medium business, or enterprise uses.

Cloud providers host services on their servers through always-on internet connections. Since their business relies on customer trust, cloud security methods are used to keep client data private and safely stored. However, cloud security also partially rests in the client's hands as well. Understanding both facets is pivotal to a healthy cloud security solution.

At its Core, Cloud Security is Composed of the Following Categories

- Data security
- Identity and access management (IAM)
- Governance (policies on threat prevention, detection, and mitigation)
- Data retention (DR) and business continuity (BC) planning
- Legal compliance

Cloud security may appear like legacy IT security, but this framework actually demands a different approach. Before diving deeper, let's first look at what cloud security is.

What is Cloud Security?

Cloud security is the whole bundle of technology, protocols, and best practices that protect cloud computing environments, applications running in the cloud, and data held in the cloud. Securing cloud services begins with understanding what exactly is being secured, as well as, the system aspects that must be managed.

As an overview, backend development against security vulnerabilities is largely within the hands of cloud service providers. Aside from choosing a security-conscious provider, clients must focus mostly on proper service configuration and safe use habits. Additionally, clients should be sure that any end-user hardware and networks are properly secured.

The full scope of cloud security is designed to protect the following, regardless of your responsibilities:

Physical networks — routers, electrical power, cabling, climate controls, etc.

Data storage — hard drives, etc.

Data servers — core network computing hardware and software

Computer virtualization frameworks — virtual machine software, host machines, and guest machines

Operating systems (OS) — software that houses

Middleware — application programming interface (API) management,

Runtime environments — execution and upkeep of a running program

Data — all the information stored, modified, and accessed

Applications — traditional software services (email, tax software, productivity suites, etc.)

End-user hardware — computers, mobile devices, Internet of Things (IoT) devices, etc.

With cloud computing, ownership over these components can vary widely. This can make the scope of client security responsibilities unclear. Since securing the cloud can look different based on who has authority over each component, it's important to understand how these are commonly grouped.

To simplify, cloud computing components are secured from two main viewpoints:

1. Cloud service types are offered by third-party providers as modules used to create the cloud environment. Depending on the type of service, you may manage a different degree of the components within the service:

The core of any third-party cloud service involves the provider managing the physical network, data storage, data servers, and computer virtualization frameworks. The service is stored on the provider's servers and virtualized via their internally managed network to be delivered to clients to be accessed remotely. This offloads hardware and other infrastructure costs to give clients access to their computing needs from anywhere via internet connectivity.

Software-as-a-Service (SaaS) cloud services provide clients access to applications that are purely hosted and run on the provider's servers. Providers manage the applications, data, runtime, middleware, and operating system. Clients are only tasked with getting their applications. SaaS examples include Google Drive, Slack, Salesforce, Microsoft 365, Cisco WebEx, Evernote.

Platform-as-a-Service cloud services provide clients a host for developing their own applications, which are run within a client's own "sandboxed" space on provider servers. Providers manage the runtime, middleware, operating system. Clients are tasked with managing their applications, data, user access, end-user devices, and end-user networks. PaaS examples include Google App Engine, Windows Azure.

Infrastructure-as-a-Service (IaaS) cloud services offer clients the hardware and remote connectivity frameworks to house the bulk of their computing, down to the operating system. Providers only manage core cloud services. Clients are tasked with securing all that gets stacked atop an operating system, including applications, data, runtimes, middleware, and the OS itself. In addition, clients need to manage user access, end-user devices, and end-user networks. IaaS examples include Microsoft Azure, Google Compute Engine (GCE), Amazon Web Services (AWS).

2. Cloud environments are deployment models in which one or more cloud services create a system for the end-users and organizations. This approach segments the management responsibilities — including security — between clients and providers.

The Currently Used Cloud Environments Are

Public cloud environments are also composed of multi-tenant cloud services where a client shares a provider's servers with other clients, like an office building or coworking space. These are third-party services run by the provider to give clients access via the web.

Private third-party cloud environments are based on the use of a cloud service that provides the client with exclusive use of their own cloud. These single-tenant environments are normally owned, managed, and operated offsite by an external provider.

Private in-house cloud environments also composed of single-tenant cloud service servers but operated from their own private data center. In this case, this cloud environment is run by the business themselves to allow full configuration and setup of every element.

Multi-cloud environments include the use of two or more cloud services from separate providers. These can be any blend of public and/or private cloud services.

Hybrid cloud environments consist of using a blend of private third-party cloud and/or onsite private cloud data center with one or more public clouds.

By framing it from this perspective, we can understand that cloud-based security can be a bit different based on the type of cloud space users are working in. But the effects are felt by both individual and organizational clients alike.

4.2 How Does Cloud Security Work?

Every cloud security measure works to accomplish one or more of the following

- Enable data recovery in case of data loss
- Protect storage and networks against malicious data theft
- Deter human error or negligence that causes data leaks
- Reduce the impact of any data or system compromise

Data security is an aspect of cloud security that involves the technical end of threat prevention. Tools and technologies allow providers and clients to insert barriers between the access and visibility of sensitive data. Among these, encryption is one of the most powerful tools available. Encryption scrambles your data so that it's only readable by someone who has the encryption key. If your data is lost or stolen, it will be effectively unreadable and meaningless. Data transit protections like virtual private networks (VPNs) are also emphasized in cloud networks.

Identity and access management (IAM) pertains to the accessibility privileges offered to user accounts. Managing authentication and authorization of user accounts also apply here. Access controls are pivotal to restrict users — both legitimate and malicious — from entering and compromising sensitive data and systems. Password management, multi-factor authentication, and other methods fall in the scope of IAM.

Governance focuses on policies for threat prevention, detection, and mitigation. With SMB and enterprises, aspects like threat intel can help with tracking and prioritizing threats to keep essential systems guarded carefully. However, even individual cloud clients could benefit from valuing safe user behavior policies and training. These apply mostly in organizational environments, but rules for safe use and response to threats can be helpful to any user.

Data retention (DR) and business continuity (BC) planning involve technical disaster recovery measures in case of data loss. Central to any DR and BC plan are methods for data redundancy such as backups. Additionally, having technical systems for ensuring uninterrupted operations can help. Frameworks for testing the validity of backups and detailed employee recovery instructions are just as valuable for a thorough BC plan.

Legal compliance revolves around protecting user privacy as set by legislative bodies. Governments have taken up the importance of protecting private user information from being exploited for profit. As such, organizations must follow regulations to abide by these policies. One approach is the use of data masking, which obscures identity within data via encryption methods.

4.3 What Makes Cloud Security Different?

Traditional IT security has felt an immense evolution due to the shift to cloud-based computing. While cloud models allow for more convenience, always-on connectivity requires new considerations to keep them secure. Cloud security, as a modernized cyber security solution, stands out from legacy IT models in a few ways.

Data storage: The biggest distinction is that older models of IT relied heavily upon onsite data storage. Organizations have long found that building all IT frameworks in-house for detailed, custom security controls is costly and rigid. Cloud-based frameworks have helped offload costs of system development and upkeep, but also remove some control from users.

Scaling speed: On a similar note, cloud security demands unique attention when scaling organization IT systems. Cloud-centric infrastructure and apps are very modular and quick to mobilize. While this ability keeps systems uniformly adjusted to organizational changes, it does pose concerns when an organization's need for upgrades and convenience outpaces their ability to keep up with security.

End-user system interfacing: For organizations and individual users alike, cloud systems also interface with many other systems and services that must be secured. Access permissions must be maintained from the end-user device level to the software level and even the network level. Beyond this, providers and users must be attentive to vulnerabilities they might cause through unsafe setup and system access behaviors.

Proximity to other networked data and systems: Since cloud systems are a persistent connection between cloud providers and all their users, this substantial network can compromise even the provider themselves. In networking landscapes, a single weak device or component can be exploited to infect the rest. Cloud providers expose themselves to threats from many end-users that they interact with, whether they are providing data storage or other services.

Additional network security responsibilities fall upon the providers who otherwise delivered products live purely on end-user systems instead of their own.

Solving most cloud security issues means that users and cloud providers — both in personal and business environments — must both remain proactive about their own roles in cyber security. This two-pronged approach means users and providers mutually must address:

Secure system configuration and maintenance.

User safety education — both behaviorally and technically.

Ultimately, cloud providers and users must have transparency and accountability to ensure both parties stay safe.

4.4 Cloud Security Risks

What are the security issues in cloud computing? Because if you don't know them, then how are you supposed to put proper measures in place? After all, weak cloud security can expose users and providers to all types of cyber security threats. Some common cloud security threats include:

Risks of cloud-based infrastructure including incompatible legacy IT frameworks, and third-party data storage service disruptions.

Internal threats due to human error such as misconfiguration of user access controls.

External threats caused almost exclusively by malicious actors, such as malware, phishing, and DDoS attacks.

The biggest risk with the cloud is that there is no perimeter. Traditional cyber security focused on protecting the perimeter, but cloud environments are highly connected which means insecure APIs (Application Programming Interfaces) and account hijacks can pose real problems. Faced with cloud computing security risks, cyber security professionals need to shift to a data-centric approach.

Interconnectedness also poses problems for networks. Malicious actors often breach networks through compromised or weak credentials. Once a hacker manages to make a landing, they can easily expand and use poorly protected interfaces in the cloud to locate data on different databases or nodes. They can even use their own cloud servers as a destination where they can export and store any stolen data. Security needs to be in the cloud — not just protecting access to your cloud data.

Third-party storage of your data and access via the internet each pose their own threats as well. If for some reason those services are interrupted, your access to the data may be lost. For instance, a phone network outage could mean you can't access the cloud at an essential time. Alternatively, a power outage could affect the data center where your data is stored, possibly with permanent data loss.

Such interruptions could have long-term repercussions. A recent power outage at an Amazon cloud data facility resulted in data loss for some customers when servers incurred hardware damage. This is a good example of why you should have local backups of at least some of your data and applications.

4.5 Why Cloud Security is Important

In the 1990s, business and personal data lived locally — and security was local as well. Data would be located on a PC's internal storage at home, and on enterprise servers, if you worked for a company.

Introducing cloud technology has forced everyone to reevaluate cyber security. Your data and applications might be floating between local and remote systems — and always internet-accessible. If you are accessing Google Docs on your smartphone, or using Salesforce software to look after your customers, that data could be held anywhere. Therefore, protecting it becomes more difficult than when it was just a question of stopping unwanted users from gaining access to your network. Cloud security requires adjusting some previous IT practices, but it has become more essential for two key reasons:

1. Convenience over security. Cloud computing is exponentially growing as a primary method for both workplace and individual use. Innovation has allowed new technology to be implemented quicker than industry security standards can keep up, putting more responsibility on users and providers to consider the risks of accessibility.
2. Centralization and multi-tenant storage. Every component — from core infrastructure to small data like emails and documents — can now be located and accessed remotely on 24/7 web-based connections. All this data gathering in the servers of a few major service providers can be highly dangerous. Threat actors can now target large multi-organizational data centers and cause immense data breaches.

Unfortunately, malicious actors realize the value of cloud-based targets and increasingly probe them for exploits. Despite cloud providers taking many security roles from clients, they do not manage everything. This leaves even non-technical users with the duty to self-educate on cloud security.

That said, users are not alone in cloud security responsibilities. Being aware of the scope of your security duties will help the entire system stay much safer.

4.6 Cloud Security Concerns – Privacy

Legislation has been put in place to help protect end users from the sale and sharing of their sensitive data. General Data Protection Regulation (GDPR) and Health Insurance Portability and Accountability Act (HIPAA) each do their own duties to protect privacy, limiting how data can be stored and accessed.

Identity management methods like data masking have been used to separate identifiable features from user data for GDPR compliance. For HIPAA compliance, organizations like healthcare facilities must make sure that their provider does their part in restricting data access as well.

The CLOUD act gives cloud providers their own legal limitations to adhere to, potentially at the cost of user privacy. US federal law now permits federal-level law enforcement to demand requested data from cloud provider servers. While this may allow investigations to proceed effectively, this may circumvent some rights to privacy and cause potential abuse of power.

How to Secure the Cloud

Fortunately, there is a lot that you can do to protect your own data in the cloud. Let's explore some of the popular methods.

Encryption is one of the best ways to secure your cloud computing systems. There are several different ways of using encryption, and they may be offered by a cloud provider or by a separate cloud security solutions provider:

- Communications encryption with the cloud in their entirety.
- Particularly sensitive data encryption, such as account credentials.
- End-to-end encryption of all data that is uploaded to the cloud.

Within the cloud, data is more at risk of being intercepted when it is on the move. When it's moving between one storage location and another, or being transmitted to your on-site application, it's vulnerable. Therefore, end-to-end encryption is the best cloud security solution for critical data. With end-to-end encryption, at no point is your communication made available to outsiders without your encryption key.

You can either encrypt your data yourself before storing it on the cloud, or you can use a cloud provider that will encrypt your data as part of the service. However, if you are only using the cloud to store non-sensitive data such as corporate graphics or videos, end-to-end encryption might be overkill. On the other hand, for financial, confidential, or commercially sensitive information, it is vital.

If you are using encryption, remember that the safe and secure management of your encryption keys is crucial. Keep a key backup and ideally don't keep it in the cloud. You might also want to change your encryption keys regularly so that if someone gains access to them, they will be locked out of the system when you make the changeover.

Configuration is another powerful practice in cloud security. Many cloud data breaches come from basic vulnerabilities such as misconfiguration errors. By preventing them, you are vastly decreasing your cloud security risk. If you don't feel confident doing this alone, you may want to consider using a separate cloud security solutions provider.

Here are a few principles you can follow:

1. Never leave the default settings unchanged. Using the default settings gives a hacker front-door access. Avoid doing this to complicate a hacker's path into your system.
2. Never leave a cloud storage bucket open. An open bucket could allow hackers to see the content just by opening the storage bucket's URL.
3. If the cloud vendor gives you security controls that you can switch on, use them. Not selecting the right security options can put you at risk.

Basic cyber security tips should also be built into any cloud implementation. Even if you are using the cloud, standard cyber security practices shouldn't be ignored. So, it is worth considering the following if you want to be as secure as possible online:

Use strong passwords. Including a mix of letters, numbers and special characters will make your password more difficult to crack. Try to avoid obvious choices, like replacing an S with a $ symbol. The more random your strings are, the better.

Use a password manager. You will be able to give each application, database, and service you use separate passwords, without having to remember them all. However, you must make sure you protect your password manager with a strong primary password.

Protect all the devices you use to access your cloud data, including smartphones and tablets. If your data is synchronized across numerous devices, any one of them could be a weak link putting your entire digital footprint at risk.

Back up your data regularly so that in the event of a cloud outage or data loss at your cloud provider, you can restore your data fully. That backup could be on your home PC, on an external hard drive, or even cloud-to-cloud, as long as you are certain the two cloud providers don't share infrastructure.

Modify permissions to prevent any individual or device from having access to all your data unless it is necessary. For instance, businesses will do this through database permission settings. If you have a home network, use guest networks for your children, for IoT devices, and for your TV. Save your 'access all areas' pass for your own usage.

Protect yourself with anti-virus and anti-malware software. Hackers can access your account easily if malware makes its way into your system.

Avoid accessing your data on public Wi-Fi, particularly if it doesn't use strong authentication. However, use a virtual private network (VPN) to protect your gateway to the cloud.

4.7 Cloud Storage and the File Sharing

Cloud computing security risks can affect everyone from businesses to individual consumers. For example, consumers can use the public cloud for storing and backing up files (using SaaS services like Dropbox), for services like email and office applications, or for doing tax forms and accounts.

If you use cloud-base services then you may need to consider how you share cloud data with others, particularly if you work as a consultant or freelancer. While sharing files on Google Drive or another service may be an easy way to share your work with clients, you may need to check that you are managing permissions properly. After all, you will want to ensure that different clients cannot see each other's names or directories or alter each other's files.

Remember that many of these commonly available cloud storage services don't encrypt data. If you want to keep your data secure through encryption, you will need to use encryption software to do it yourself before you upload the data. You will then have to give your clients a key, or they won't be able to read the files.

Check Your Cloud Provider's Security

Security should be one of the main points to consider when it comes to choosing a cloud security provider. That's because your cyber security is no longer just your responsibility: cloud security companies must do their part in creating a secure cloud environment — and share the responsibility for data security.

Unfortunately, cloud companies are not going to give you the blueprints to their network security. This would be equivalent to a bank providing you with details of their vault — complete with the combination numbers to the safe.

However, getting the right answers to some basic questions gives you better confidence that your cloud assets will be safe. In addition, you will be more aware of whether your provider has properly addressed obvious cloud security risks. We recommend asking your cloud provider some questions of the following questions:

Security audits: "Do you conduct regular external audits of your security?"

Data segmentation: "Is customer data is logically segmented and kept separate?"

Encryption: "Is our data encrypted? What parts of it are encrypted?"

Customer data retention: "What customer data retention policies are being followed?"

User data retention: "Is my data is properly deleted if I leave your cloud service?"

Access management: "How are access rights controlled?"

You will also want to make sure you've read your provider's terms of service (TOS). Reading the TOS is essential to understanding if you are receiving exactly what you want and need.

Be sure to check that you also know all the services used with your provider. If your files are on Dropbox or backed up on iCloud (Apple's storage cloud), that may well mean they are actually held on Amazon's servers. So, you will need to check out AWS, as well as, the service you are using directly.

4.8 Hybrid Cloud Security Solutions

Hybrid cloud security services can be a very smart choice for clients in SMB and enterprise spaces. They are most viable for SMB and enterprise applications since they are generally too complex for personal use. But it's these organizations that could use the blend of scale and accessibility of the cloud with onsite control of specific data.

Here are a few security benefits of hybrid cloud security systems:

Segmentation of services can help an organization control how their data is accessed and stored. For example, placing more sensitive data onsite while offloading other data, applications, and processes into the cloud can help you layer your security appropriately. In addition, separating data can improve your organization's ability to remain legally compliant with data regulations.

Redundancy can also be accomplished via hybrid cloud environments. By utilizing daily operations from public cloud servers and backing up systems in local data servers, organizations can keep their operations moving in the case that one data center is taken offline or infected with ransomware.

4.9 SMB Cloud Security Solutions

While enterprises can insist on a private cloud — the internet equivalent of owning your own office building or campus — individuals and smaller businesses must manage with public cloud services. This is like sharing a serviced office or living in an apartment block with hundreds of other tenants. Therefore, your security needs to be a prime concern.

In small to medium business applications, you will find cloud security is largely on the public providers you use.

However, there are measures you can take to keep yourself safe:

Multi-tenant data segmentation: Businesses must be sure that their data cannot be accessed by any other clients of their cloud vendors. Whether housed in segmented servers, or carefully encrypted, be sure segmentation measures are in place.

User access controls: Controlling permissions might mean throttling user access to an inconvenient level. However, going restrictive and working backward to find a balance can be much safer than allowing loose permissions to permeate your network.

Legal data compliance: Keeping your data compliant with international regulations like GDPR is critical to avoid heavy fines and reputation damage. Make sure measures like data masking and classification of sensitive data is a priority for your organization.

Careful scaling of cloud systems: With the rapid implementation of cloud systems, be sure you take time to check your organization's systems for security over convenience. Cloud services can quickly become sprawling to the point of lacking regulation.

4.10 Enterprise Cloud Security Solutions

Since cloud computing is now used by over 90% of larger enterprises, cloud security is a vital part of corporate cyber security. Private cloud services and other more costly infrastructure may be viable for enterprise-level organizations. However, you will still have to ensure your internal IT is on top of maintaining the entire surface area of your networks.

For large-scale enterprise use, cloud security can be far more flexible if you make some investments into your infrastructure.

There Are a Few Key Takeaways to Keep in Mind

Actively manage your accounts and services: If you don't use a service or software anymore, close it down properly. Hackers can gain easy access to an entire cloud network via old, dormant accounts through unpatched vulnerabilities.

Multi-factor authentication (MFA): This could be biometric data such as fingerprints, or a password and separate code sent to your mobile device. It is time-consuming, but useful for your most sensitive data.

Evaluate the cost-benefits of hybrid cloud: Segmenting your data is far more important in enterprise use, as you will be handling much larger quantities of data. You need to make sure your data is separate from other customers' data, whether it's separately encrypted or logically segmented for separate storage. Hybrid cloud services can help with this.

Be wary of shadow IT: Educating your employees to avoid using unauthorized cloud services on your networks or for company work is essential. If sensitive data is communicated over unsecured channels, your organization may be exposed to malicious actors or legal issues.

So, whether you are an individual user, SMB user, or even Enterprise level cloud user — it is important to make sure that your network and devices are as secure as possible. This starts with having a good understanding of basic cyber security on an individual user level, as well as, ensuring that your network and all devices are protected using a robust security solution that is built for the cloud.

Chapter 5

The Modern Network Landscape and the Security Imperative

5.1 Introduction

The enterprise network has undergone a fundamental transformation over the past two decades. What once consisted of predictable data flows between branch offices and centralized data centers has evolved into a complex, distributed ecosystem where applications reside in multiple clouds, users work from anywhere, and data traverses numerous networks before reaching its destination. This transformation, driven by digital innovation and competitive pressures, has brought unprecedented agility and capability to organizations. However, it has also introduced profound security challenges that traditional networking and security architectures struggle to address.

This chapter explores the evolution of enterprise networking from traditional MPLS-based architectures to today's cloud-centric, distributed environments. We examine how digital transformation has eliminated the traditional network perimeter, creating new attack surfaces and threat vectors that adversaries eagerly exploit. We introduce Software-Defined Wide Area Networking (SD-WAN) as a transformative technology that addresses many networking challenges of the modern era. Finally, we confront a critical reality: while SD-WAN solves important networking problems, it alone cannot address the security imperatives of today's threat landscape, necessitating an integrated approach that combines networking and security from the ground up.

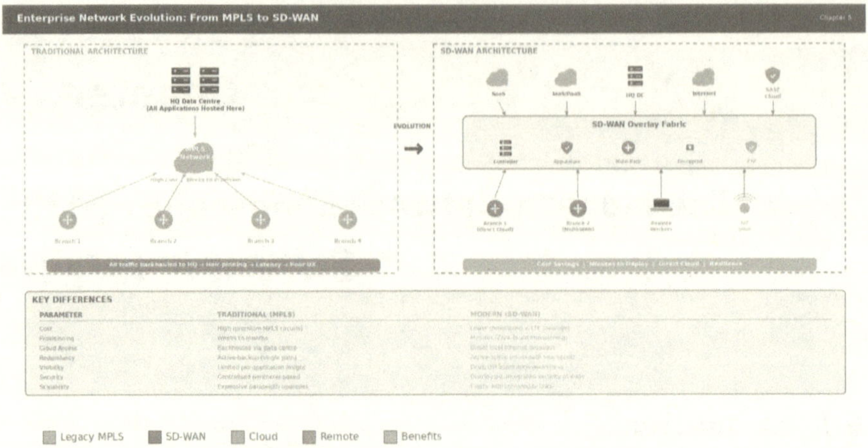

Figure 5.1: Enterprise Network Evolution — From MPLS to SD-WAN

5.2 The Evolution of the Enterprise Network: From MPLS to the Cloud

The Traditional Enterprise Network Architecture

For decades, enterprise networking followed a relatively straightforward model. Organizations operated from fixed locations—headquarters, regional offices, branch locations, and manufacturing facilities. Users came to the office each day, logged into desktop computers, and accessed applications hosted in corporate data centers. Network traffic followed predictable patterns: it flowed from branches through hub sites to centralized data centers where applications and data resided.

This traditional architecture relied heavily on Multi-Protocol Label Switching (MPLS) technology. MPLS provided reliable, predictable performance by creating private network paths through service provider infrastructure. An MPLS network functioned like a private highway system for corporate data, ensuring that packets traveled efficiently and securely between locations without traversing the public internet. Service providers guaranteed performance through

Service Level Agreements (SLAs) that specified uptime, latency, jitter, and packet loss metrics.

The MPLS model offered significant advantages for its time. It provided consistent, high-quality connectivity ideal for latency-sensitive applications like voice over IP (VoIP) and video conferencing. The private nature of MPLS circuits meant that data never traversed the public internet, providing inherent security through isolation. Traffic engineering capabilities allowed network administrators to prioritize critical applications and ensure optimal use of expensive WAN bandwidth. For organizations with relatively static network topologies and centralized application architectures, MPLS delivered exactly what was needed.

The Limitations of MPLS in a Changing World

As enterprise computing began its inexorable shift toward the cloud, the limitations of MPLS-based architectures became increasingly apparent. The first challenge was economic. MPLS circuits commanded premium pricing compared to commodity internet connectivity. A 100 Mbps MPLS connection might cost ten to twenty times more than an equivalent internet circuit. For organizations with dozens or hundreds of locations, these costs accumulated rapidly, consuming substantial portions of IT budgets.

The second challenge was agility—or more precisely, the lack thereof. Provisioning new MPLS circuits typically required weeks or even months. Service providers needed to provision circuits, configure routers, and coordinate installation activities. For organizations attempting to open new offices quickly, acquire companies, or respond to rapid business changes, these timelines proved frustratingly slow. In an era where cloud infrastructure could be provisioned in minutes, waiting months for connectivity felt anachronistic.

Bandwidth scalability presented a third challenge. MPLS pricing increased significantly with bandwidth. While a 10 Mbps circuit might be affordable, upgrading to 100 Mbps or 1 Gbps could prove prohibitively expensive, especially for smaller branch locations. Yet bandwidth demands were exploding. High-definition video conferencing, cloud application adoption, and the proliferation of connected devices all drove insatiable appetite for bandwidth. Organizations found themselves in an impossible bind: user expectations demanded more bandwidth, but budget realities constrained MPLS expansion.

The Cloud Computing Revolution

The emergence of cloud computing fundamentally disrupted traditional networking models. Software-as-a-Service (SaaS) applications like Salesforce, Microsoft 365, and Workday moved critical business functions from corporate data centers to providers' clouds. Infrastructure-as-a-Service (IaaS) platforms like Amazon Web Services (AWS), Microsoft Azure, and Google Cloud Platform enabled organizations to build and deploy applications in provider data centers around the world. Platform-as-a-Service (PaaS) offerings provided development frameworks and services that accelerated application delivery.

This shift had profound implications for networking. Suddenly, significant volumes of traffic needed to reach destinations on the public internet rather than corporate data centers. Branch office users accessing Office 365 or Salesforce generated traffic that, in a traditional hub-and-spoke MPLS architecture, would backhaul through the corporate data center before breaking out to the internet. This "hair-pinning" of traffic introduced unnecessary latency, consumed expensive MPLS bandwidth, and degraded user experience. It made no sense for a branch office user to send traffic hundreds or thousands of miles to a data center, only to have it traverse back across the internet to reach a cloud application hosted near the branch location.

Organizations responded by establishing local internet breakouts at branch locations, allowing cloud-bound traffic to reach its destination directly. However, this approach introduced security concerns. Traditional security architectures positioned firewalls, intrusion prevention systems, and other security appliances at the data center, protecting traffic as it entered and exited the corporate network. Direct internet breakouts bypassed these controls, potentially exposing users and devices to internet-borne threats.

The Hybrid and Multi-Cloud Reality

Few organizations moved entirely to the cloud. Instead, most adopted hybrid architectures that combined on-premises infrastructure with cloud services. Legacy applications remained in corporate data centers due to technical constraints, regulatory requirements, or simple economics. Modern applications ran in public clouds, taking advantage of scale, resilience, and advanced services. This hybrid reality meant that traffic patterns became increasingly complex and unpredictable.

Multi-cloud strategies added further complexity. Organizations adopted multiple cloud providers for various reasons: avoiding vendor lock-in, leveraging best-of-breed services, or supporting acquired companies' existing platforms. An enterprise might run SAP in its own data center, host customer-facing web applications in AWS, use Microsoft 365 and Azure for productivity and development, and deploy specialized AI workloads on Google Cloud Platform. Each platform introduced unique networking and connectivity requirements.

The traditional hub-and-spoke MPLS model, designed for predictable traffic patterns between fixed locations, proved fundamentally unsuited to this new reality. A more flexible, dynamic approach was required—one that could route traffic efficiently regardless of source or destination, leverage diverse connectivity options, and adapt quickly to changing business requirements.

5.3 Distributed Workloads and the Perimeterless Network: SaaS, IaaS, and Hybrid IT

The Dissolution of the Network Perimeter

The concept of a network perimeter has been central to information security for decades. Traditional security models assumed that threats existed "outside" the corporate network while trusted users and systems resided "inside." Firewalls served as gatekeepers, inspecting traffic at the perimeter and blocking malicious activity while allowing legitimate business traffic to flow. This castle-and-moat approach worked reasonably well when the perimeter was well-defined and relatively static.

Cloud computing, mobile workforces, and digital transformation have rendered this perimeter-based model obsolete. Today's enterprise is fundamentally perimeterless. Applications run in multiple clouds and on-premises data centers. Users work from home offices, coffee shops, airports, and hotel rooms. Contractors, partners, and customers access corporate resources from their own networks and devices. Data flows across multiple networks, providers, and geographic regions before reaching its destination. The clear boundary between "inside" and "outside" has dissolved.

This perimeterless reality has profound security implications. When the perimeter was well-defined, organizations could concentrate security resources at specific chokepoints. Today, every endpoint, every application, and every network connection represents a potential entry point for attackers. The attack surface has expanded exponentially, while the ability to control and monitor that surface has diminished.

Software-as-a-Service and the SaaS Sprawl Challenge

Software-as-a-Service represents perhaps the most visible manifestation of cloud computing. Organizations have eagerly adopted SaaS applications for virtually every business function. Salesforce handles customer relationship management. Workday manages human resources and finance. Slack facilitates team collaboration. Zoom enables video communication. ServiceNow automates IT operations. The list grows continuously as vendors migrate applications to the cloud and new cloud-native solutions emerge.

This SaaS proliferation creates what security professionals call "SaaS sprawl." The average enterprise uses hundreds of distinct SaaS applications, many adopted without central IT involvement or approval. Business units, tired of slow IT procurement processes, simply provide credit card information and begin using whatever services meet their needs. This "shadow IT" phenomenon means that IT and security teams often lack visibility into what applications employees use, what data resides in those applications, and what security controls protect that data.

Each SaaS application introduces unique security considerations. What authentication mechanisms does it support? How does it encrypt data in transit and at rest? What compliance certifications has it obtained? How does it handle data residency and sovereignty requirements? What visibility does it provide into user activities? Can it integrate with corporate identity systems and security tools? Organizations struggle to answer these questions for the dozens or hundreds of SaaS applications their employees use.

From a networking perspective, SaaS applications generate substantial volumes of traffic destined for the internet rather than corporate data centers. Users expect fast, reliable access to these applications regardless of their location. Routing this traffic through traditional backhauling architectures introduces unacceptable latency and bandwidth consumption. Yet providing direct internet access at every location raises security concerns about exposing users to internet-borne threats.

Infrastructure-as-a-Service and Hybrid Cloud Architectures

Infrastructure-as-a-Service platforms like AWS, Azure, and Google Cloud Platform provide organizations with on-demand compute, storage, and networking resources. Rather than purchasing and maintaining physical servers, organizations provision virtual machines, containers, and serverless functions in provider data centers. This approach offers numerous advantages: rapid provisioning, elastic scaling, global availability, and consumption-based pricing.

However, IaaS introduces significant networking complexity. Organizations typically deploy workloads across multiple availability zones and regions for resilience and performance. These workloads need connectivity to corporate networks for access to on-premises systems and data. They need connectivity to SaaS applications. They need connectivity to other cloud environments in multi-cloud architectures. They need secure connectivity for administrators and users accessing cloud-hosted applications.

Hybrid architectures that combine on-premises and cloud infrastructure create particularly complex networking requirements. An e-commerce application might run its web front-end in AWS for scalability, while maintaining its customer database on-premises for compliance reasons. Processing a customer order requires rapid, reliable communication between cloud and on-premises components. High latency or network instability directly impacts application performance and user experience.

Each cloud provider offers native networking services with unique characteristics and limitations. AWS uses Virtual Private Clouds (VPCs) with specific routing and security group configurations. Azure implements Virtual Networks with network security groups and service endpoints. Google Cloud Platform provides VPC networks with its own routing and firewall mechanisms. Organizations attempting to maintain consistent networking and security policies across multiple clouds face a daunting challenge of understanding and operationalizing these provider-specific implementations.

The Remote and Mobile Workforce

The shift to remote work, accelerated dramatically by global events but already underway for years, has fundamentally altered where users access corporate resources. No longer do employees reliably connect from corporate offices with managed network connections. Instead, they work from home offices using residential broadband, from hotels using untrusted WiFi, or from mobile devices using cellular connections. This distributed workforce demands access to the same applications and data they would access from the office, with equivalent performance and security.

Traditional VPN technology provided remote access for traveling executives and occasional remote workers. Users would establish encrypted tunnels from their devices to corporate VPN concentrators, gaining access to internal resources as if physically present in the office. However, VPN architectures struggle when remote work becomes the norm rather than the exception. VPN concentrators become bottlenecks as thousands of users simultaneously connect. Backhauling all traffic through the corporate data center introduces latency and bandwidth constraints. The "connected to VPN" or "disconnected from VPN" binary model provides inadequate granularity for modern security requirements.

Furthermore, remote users typically access cloud applications more frequently than on-premises applications. Forcing all their traffic through a VPN tunnel to the corporate data center, only to have it break out to the internet to reach a cloud application, makes little sense. Yet allowing unsecured direct access to cloud applications bypasses security controls and creates visibility gaps.

The Internet of Things and Operational Technology

Digital transformation extends beyond IT systems to encompass operational technology (OT) and the Internet of Things (IoT). Manufacturing facilities deploy sensors and controllers connected to networks. Retail stores use connected point-of-sale systems, digital signage, and inventory management devices. Healthcare facilities operate medical devices and building management systems. Smart city initiatives connect traffic systems, utility infrastructure, and public safety equipment.

These IoT and OT devices introduce unique security challenges. Many lack basic security capabilities, running outdated operating systems without security updates. They often use default or weak credentials. They may communicate using unencrypted protocols. Yet they connect to networks and, in many cases, to the internet, creating potential attack vectors. The 2016 Mirai botnet, which compromised hundreds of thousands of IoT devices and launched devastating distributed denial-of-service attacks, demonstrated the severity of this threat.

From a networking perspective, IoT and OT devices often require specialized connectivity. They may use non-IP protocols, operate on isolated networks for safety reasons, or have strict latency and reliability requirements. Integrating these devices into enterprise networks while maintaining appropriate segmentation and security controls adds yet another layer of complexity.

5.4 The Security Challenge in the Digital Transformation Era: New Attack Surfaces and Threat Vectors

The Expanding Attack Surface

The combination of cloud computing, distributed workloads, remote workforces, and proliferating connected devices has created an exponentially expanded attack surface. Every endpoint, application, network connection, and data repository represents a potential target for adversaries. Traditional security models that focused on protecting a well-defined perimeter prove inadequate when the perimeter has effectively disappeared.

Consider the attack surface of a typical modern enterprise. Corporate data centers host legacy applications and infrastructure. Multiple cloud platforms host new applications and workloads. SaaS applications store sensitive corporate data in vendor-managed environments. Remote employees access resources from home networks and mobile devices. Branch offices maintain local internet connections. Partners and contractors require selective access to corporate resources. IoT devices connect from operational environments. Each of these components creates opportunities for compromise.

The interconnected nature of modern environments means that compromise of one component can cascade to others. An attacker who gains access to a user's laptop through a phishing email might pivot to cloud environments using cached credentials. Compromising a vulnerable IoT device might provide a foothold for lateral movement to more valuable systems. Exploiting a misconfigured cloud storage bucket might expose customer data that enables further attacks. The attack surface is not merely large—it is dynamic, interconnected, and difficult to inventory comprehensively.

Sophisticated Threat Actors and Advanced Persistent Threats

The threat landscape has evolved as dramatically as the technology landscape. Today's adversaries range from opportunistic criminals to well-funded, highly sophisticated nation-state actors. Advanced Persistent Threats (APTs) employ multi-stage attacks that unfold over months or years, patiently establishing footholds, escalating privileges, and exfiltrating data while evading detection.

These sophisticated actors continuously adapt their techniques to exploit weaknesses in modern architectures. They understand that cloud environments often suffer from configuration errors and overly permissive access controls. They recognize that remote workers may use personal devices with inadequate security. They know that security teams struggle with visibility across distributed environments. They exploit the complexity that results from rapid digital transformation and the adoption of new technologies faster than security processes can adapt.

Ransomware represents perhaps the most visible threat, with attacks increasingly targeting critical infrastructure, healthcare providers, and essential services. Modern ransomware operators conduct reconnaissance to identify valuable targets, exfiltrate data before encryption to enable double extortion, and specifically target backup systems to eliminate recovery options. The professionalization of the ransomware ecosystem, with ransomware-as-a-service offerings and specialized affiliates, has industrialized this threat.

Cloud-Specific Threats and Misconfiguration Risks

Cloud environments introduce unique security challenges distinct from traditional on-premises infrastructure. The shared responsibility model, where cloud providers secure the underlying infrastructure while customers secure their workloads and data, creates potential gaps when organizations misunderstand their responsibilities. Misconfigurations represent the most common source of cloud security incidents, from publicly accessible storage buckets to overly permissive identity policies.

The dynamic, API-driven nature of cloud environments enables rapid provisioning but also creates security risks. Developers can spin up resources in minutes without security review. Automated deployment pipelines might introduce vulnerabilities into production. The ephemeral nature of cloud resources—containers that exist for minutes, serverless functions that execute and terminate—challenges traditional security tools designed for persistent infrastructure.

Credential theft and abuse plague cloud environments. If attackers obtain cloud access credentials or API keys, they can authenticate legitimately to cloud platforms and operate undetected. Traditional perimeter-based security controls cannot prevent this access because the attackers appear as authorized users. Sophisticated attackers specifically target cloud credentials, knowing that a compromised cloud administrator account provides vast access to data and systems.

The Insider Threat and Privileged Access Abuse

While external attackers receive the most attention, insider threats—whether malicious or negligent—pose significant risks. Employees with authorized access might intentionally steal data, sabotage systems, or facilitate external attacks. More commonly, well-meaning employees might inadvertently compromise security through poor practices, social engineering victimization, or simple errors.

The challenge intensifies in distributed, cloud-centric environments where users have broad access to systems and data. A developer with access to production cloud environments might accidentally expose sensitive data. A contractor might leave access credentials in a public code repository. An executive might fall victim to a sophisticated spear-phishing attack and provide credentials to attackers. Traditional security controls often struggle to distinguish authorized users behaving abnormally from normal user activity.

Privileged accounts—those with administrative access to systems, applications, or data—represent particularly attractive targets. Compromise of a privileged account can provide attackers with the keys to the kingdom, enabling them to access any system, exfiltrate any data, or deploy ransomware across the entire environment. Yet organizations struggle to manage and monitor privileged access effectively, especially across multiple cloud platforms with different identity and access management implementations.

Supply Chain and Third-Party Risks

Modern organizations rely on extensive ecosystems of suppliers, partners, and service providers. Each external party that requires access to corporate systems or data extends the attack surface. Supply chain attacks, where adversaries compromise software or services provided by trusted vendors, have proven devastatingly effective. The SolarWinds attack, which compromised software updates and enabled access to thousands of organizations including government agencies, demonstrated the catastrophic potential of supply chain compromise.

Third-party risk extends beyond software supply chains. Managed service providers require access to customer environments. Partners need connectivity for business-critical integrations. Contractors use their own devices to access corporate resources. Each of these relationships creates potential security gaps, yet organizations often lack visibility into third-party security practices or the ability to enforce security requirements on external parties.

The Challenge of Encryption and Visibility

Encryption has become ubiquitous, protecting data in transit from interception and tampering. Over 90% of internet traffic now uses encryption, and the percentage continues to rise. While this represents a significant security improvement in many respects, it creates challenges for security monitoring and threat detection. Traditional security tools that rely on inspecting network traffic struggle when that traffic is encrypted.

Attackers understand this limitation and increasingly use encryption to hide their activities. Malware might communicate with command-and-control servers over encrypted channels. Data exfiltration might occur through encrypted tunnels that blend with legitimate traffic. Without the ability to inspect encrypted traffic, security tools operate with reduced effectiveness, potentially missing critical threats.

Organizations face difficult tradeoffs. They can decrypt and inspect traffic, but this requires significant computational resources, introduces latency, and raises privacy concerns. They can deploy tools at endpoints to inspect traffic before encryption, but this requires managing agents across diverse devices and environments. They can focus on metadata and behavioral analytics rather than packet-level inspection, but this may miss certain attack types. No approach fully resolves the tension between encryption and visibility.

5.5 Introducing Software-Defined Wide Area Networking (SD-WAN): Core Concepts, Benefits, and Architecture

1. The Fundamental Concept of SD-WAN

Software-Defined Wide Area Networking emerged as a response to the limitations of traditional WAN architectures in cloud-centric environments. At its core, SD-WAN separates the control plane—the intelligence that makes routing decisions—from the data plane—the actual forwarding of packets. This separation, similar to software-defined networking (SDN) concepts applied to data centers, enables centralized management and dynamic, policy-based routing across diverse connectivity types.

Traditional routers combine control and data planes in single devices configured individually. If an organization operates 100 branch locations, network administrators must configure 100 routers, often manually or using complex scripts. Policy changes require touching each device. Troubleshooting involves logging into individual routers to examine configuration and status. This model becomes increasingly unwieldy as networks grow and change frequently.

SD-WAN centralizes the control plane, allowing administrators to define policies once and have them automatically implemented across all locations. The data plane—SD-WAN appliances or software at each location—receives instructions from the centralized controller and forwards traffic accordingly. This architecture dramatically simplifies management while enabling sophisticated routing capabilities that would be impractical to configure manually.

2. Transport Independence and Multi-Path Capabilities

One of SD-WAN's most significant advantages is transport independence. Traditional WAN architectures typically relied exclusively on MPLS circuits. SD-WAN can leverage any connectivity available—MPLS, broadband internet, LTE/5G cellular, satellite—treating each as a potential path for traffic. This transport independence enables organizations to reduce costs by supplementing or replacing expensive MPLS circuits with more affordable options while maintaining or even improving reliability.

SD-WAN implements intelligent traffic steering across multiple paths simultaneously. Rather than designating one circuit as primary and others as backup, SD-WAN can actively utilize all available paths, selecting the optimal path for each application flow based on real-time conditions and policy requirements. Latency-sensitive voice traffic might use the lowest-latency path. Bulk data transfers might use the highest-bandwidth path. Mission-critical applications might use the most reliable path, as determined by continuous monitoring.

This multi-path capability provides inherent resilience. If one circuit fails or degrades, SD-WAN automatically redirects traffic to alternate paths within subsequent timeframes, typically faster than users notice any disruption. Unlike traditional architectures where circuit failures cause significant downtime until providers repair the connection, SD-WAN's use of diverse transports means that multiple simultaneous failures would be required to completely isolate a location.

3. Application Awareness and Quality of Service

Traditional routing makes forwarding decisions based on destination IP addresses, treating all traffic to a given destination identically. SD-WAN introduces application awareness, identifying specific applications and treating their traffic according to policies that consider the application's requirements and business priority. An SD-WAN system might recognize Office 365 traffic and give it priority over general web browsing. It might steer Salesforce traffic to a low-latency path while sending backup traffic over a high-bandwidth but higher-latency path.

This application awareness relies on various identification techniques. Deep packet inspection examines packet contents to identify application signatures. Machine learning analyzes traffic patterns and behaviors to classify applications. Integration with cloud provider APIs enables direct identification of traffic destined for specific cloud services. The combination of techniques allows SD-WAN to accurately identify and classify applications even when they use dynamic IP addresses or encrypted connections.

Quality of Service (QoS) capabilities ensure that critical applications receive necessary network resources. When multiple applications compete for limited bandwidth, SD-WAN prioritizes traffic according to policy. Voice and video conferencing might receive guaranteed bandwidth and low latency. Business-critical applications might receive priority over recreational internet use. During periods of congestion, less important traffic might be rate-limited to ensure that priority applications maintain acceptable performance.

4. Zero-Touch Provisioning and Simplified Operations

SD-WAN dramatically simplifies the operational aspects of WAN management through zero-touch provisioning (ZTP) and centralized management. When an organization opens a new location, the traditional approach required scheduling technician visits, manually configuring routers, and coordinating with service providers—a process consuming weeks. SD-WAN enables a fundamentally different approach.

With ZTP, an organization ships a pre-configured SD-WAN appliance to the new location. An on-site employee with no networking expertise connects the device to available internet circuits and powers it on. The appliance automatically contacts the centralized SD-WAN controller, downloads its configuration, and establishes secure connectivity to other locations. The entire process completes in minutes without specialized technical resources. This capability proves particularly valuable for retail chains, distributed enterprises, or organizations experiencing rapid growth.

Centralized management extends beyond initial provisioning. Network administrators can view the entire WAN from a single interface, monitoring the status of all locations, circuits, and applications. Policy changes apply globally or to specific groups of locations without touching individual devices. Troubleshooting becomes significantly simpler when administrators can examine network-wide data rather than piecing together information from hundreds of individual devices. Reporting and analytics provide insights into network utilization, application performance, and potential issues.

5. Architectural Components and Deployment Models

An SD-WAN architecture consists of several key components. Edge devices—whether physical appliances, virtual machines, or software running on universal customer premises equipment (uCPE)—reside at each location, forwarding traffic according to centralized policies. These edge devices establish secure overlay networks, typically using encrypted tunnels across multiple underlay transports.

The SD-WAN controller provides centralized policy definition, configuration management, and orchestration. In some architectures, the controller actively participates in packet forwarding decisions. In others, it programs edge devices with policies that they implement independently. Cloud-based controllers offer particular advantages, eliminating the need for organizations to maintain controller infrastructure while ensuring high availability and global accessibility.

SD-WAN gateways or cloud points-of-presence enable optimized connectivity to cloud platforms and internet destinations. Rather than backhauling branch office traffic to a data center for internet breakout, branches can connect directly to nearby SD-WAN gateways that provide optimized paths to cloud applications and internet services. These gateways often incorporate security services, enabling branches to access the internet securely without backhauling traffic through data center security appliances.

Organizations can deploy SD-WAN in various models. A greenfield deployment replaces existing WAN infrastructure entirely with SD-WAN. A brownfield or hybrid deployment supplements existing MPLS networks with SD-WAN, allowing gradual migration. Some organizations use SD-WAN exclusively for internet connectivity while maintaining MPLS for critical applications. The flexibility of SD-WAN architecture accommodates diverse organizational requirements and migration strategies.

6. Key Benefits of SD-WAN Adoption

The benefits of SD-WAN adoption extend across cost, performance, agility, and user experience dimensions. Cost reductions typically represent the most immediately tangible benefit. By leveraging broadband internet and LTE connectivity instead of expensive MPLS circuits, organizations commonly reduce WAN costs by 30-60%. The ability to scale bandwidth affordably means that branch offices can have 10x or even 100x the bandwidth at equivalent or lower cost.

Performance improvements result from intelligent traffic steering and optimization. Applications receive the network characteristics they require—low latency for voice, high bandwidth for data, reliability for critical systems. Direct internet breakouts reduce latency for cloud applications by 40-60% compared to backhauling through data centers. Multi-path capabilities ensure that degradation of one circuit doesn't impact application performance.

Operational agility improvements enable organizations to respond quickly to business needs. Opening new locations, implementing acquisitions, or adjusting to changing requirements happens in days rather than months. Centralized management reduces the administrative burden of WAN operations, allowing network teams to focus on strategic initiatives rather than routine device configuration.

User experience improvements manifest in faster application access, reduced downtime, and consistent performance regardless of location.

Employees in branch offices receive the same quality of connectivity as headquarters users. Remote workers can access corporate resources reliably. The business outcomes—improved productivity, customer satisfaction, and competitive advantage—justify SD-WAN investments even beyond direct cost savings.

5.6 Why SD-WAN Alone is Not Enough: The Need for Integrated, Built-In Security

1. The Security Gaps in Basic SD-WAN

While SD-WAN addresses many networking challenges, it does not inherently solve the security challenges discussed earlier in this chapter. Basic SD-WAN focuses on connectivity, performance, and management—not security. Early SD-WAN implementations often provided minimal security capabilities, primarily offering encrypted tunnels between locations to protect data in transit. While this encryption prevents eavesdropping on WAN traffic, it addresses only one aspect of a comprehensive security strategy.

The fundamental issue is architectural. SD-WAN establishes connectivity—effectively building high-performance highways between locations and to cloud resources. However, connectivity without security controls is like building highways without traffic laws, signals, or enforcement. Traffic flows efficiently, but dangerous drivers can cause harm without constraint. Organizations need both connectivity and security, tightly integrated to enable business while preventing attacks.

Consider a branch office using SD-WAN with direct internet breakout for performance optimization. Users gain fast access to cloud applications, meeting the performance objective. However, if the SD-WAN implementation lacks integrated security, those users directly access the internet without firewall protection, intrusion prevention, web filtering, or malware defense. A user who clicks a malicious link can compromise their device and, through lateral movement, potentially compromise other systems. The connectivity improvement inadvertently increases risk.

2. The Bolt-On Security Challenge

Recognizing the security limitations of basic SD-WAN, many organizations attempt to bolt on security capabilities. They might deploy firewalls at each branch office alongside SD-WAN appliances. They might backhaul some traffic to data centers for security inspection while allowing other traffic to break out locally. They might deploy cloud-based security services that SD-WAN tunnels traffic through. While these approaches can work, they introduce significant challenges.

Bolt-on security typically requires deploying, managing, and maintaining separate products from different vendors. Each product has its own management interface, logging format, and operational procedures. Network teams manage SD-WAN while security teams manage security appliances, creating potential coordination gaps. Troubleshooting becomes complex when issues might stem from SD-WAN configuration, security policies, or their interaction.

Performance can suffer with bolt-on approaches. Traffic must traverse multiple devices—perhaps exiting an SD-WAN appliance, passing through a firewall, undergoing inspection by a threat prevention system, and then continuing its journey. Each hop adds latency. If security devices become bottlenecks, they constrain bandwidth regardless of the underlying connectivity. The performance benefits of SD-WAN can be negated by security infrastructure that cannot keep pace.

Cost implications deserve consideration. Organizations must purchase, deploy, and maintain separate security appliances at each location. They must allocate budget for multiple vendor relationships, support contracts, and training. The total cost of ownership for bolt-on security can be substantial, potentially eroding the cost savings that motivated SD-WAN adoption in the first place.

3. The Cloud Security Service Insertion Challenge

Another common approach involves redirecting traffic from SD-WAN to cloud-based security services. Traffic from a branch office might tunnel to a cloud security platform, undergo inspection, and then proceed to its destination. This model, sometimes called security service edge or secure web gateway, offers advantages over appliance-based approaches. The security services scale elastically, don't require per-location hardware, and update automatically.

However, service insertion introduces its own challenges. Traffic must detour through security service points-of-presence, potentially adding latency and impacting performance. If the security service location is not optimally positioned relative to the traffic source and destination, the detour might be substantial. During security service outages or connectivity issues to the service, traffic flow can be disrupted.

The split responsibility between SD-WAN for connectivity and cloud services for security creates operational complexity. Administrators must coordinate configuration across separate systems. Troubleshooting requires examining multiple platforms. Ensuring consistent policies across all traffic types and locations becomes challenging when policies are defined in different systems with different models.

4. The Need for Convergence: Secure SD-WAN

The limitations of basic SD-WAN and bolt-on security approaches led to the emergence of secure SD-WAN—solutions that integrate networking and security capabilities in unified platforms. This convergence addresses the fundamental reality that networking and security are inseparable in modern environments. Every network design decision has security implications, and every security control affects network performance and user experience. Attempting to maintain them as separate domains creates friction, gaps, and operational complexity.

Secure SD-WAN integrates security functions directly into the SD-WAN architecture. Firewalling, intrusion prevention, web filtering, malware defense, and other security capabilities operate on the same platform that provides connectivity. This integration offers numerous advantages. Management occurs through a single interface with consistent policies across networking and security domains. Troubleshooting benefits from unified visibility. Performance optimization considers both connectivity and security requirements. The same platform that intelligently routes traffic also protects it.

The security capabilities in secure SD-WAN must be comprehensive and enterprise-grade. Basic stateful firewalling proves insufficient in today's threat landscape. Organizations require next-generation firewall capabilities that identify applications, users, and content. Intrusion prevention must detect and block sophisticated attacks. Web filtering should prevent access to malicious sites. Anti-malware capabilities need to inspect files and detect known and unknown threats. Advanced threat prevention should employ sandboxing and behavioral analysis. DNS security can prevent connections to malicious domains.

5. The Importance of Consistent Policy Enforcement

One of secure SD-WAN's most significant benefits is consistent policy enforcement across all locations and users. In traditional architectures with different security appliances at different locations, policy inconsistencies are common. Branch offices might have less sophisticated security than headquarters. Remote users might have different controls than office-based users. Newly opened locations might lack proper security during initial deployment. Each inconsistency creates potential attack vectors.

Secure SD-WAN enables organizations to define security policies centrally and enforce them universally. A policy that blocks access to high-risk websites applies equally at headquarters, branch offices, and for remote users. Security updates and threat intelligence automatically distribute to all enforcement points. When threat researchers identify new attack signatures, protection deploys everywhere simultaneously rather than requiring manual updates to hundreds of appliances.

This consistency extends to granular policy definition based on context. Policies can consider user identity, device security posture, location, time of day, data sensitivity, and application characteristics. An executive accessing financial systems from a corporate device on the corporate network might receive full access. The same executive accessing the same systems from a personal device over public WiFi might face additional authentication requirements and restrictions. These context-aware policies enable organizations to balance security and usability appropriately.

6. Cloud-Native Architecture and Scalability

Modern secure SD-WAN solutions increasingly adopt cloud-native architectures that leverage the scale and resilience of cloud platforms. Rather than requiring organizations to maintain on-premises controllers and security infrastructure, cloud-delivered solutions provide these capabilities as services. This approach offers significant advantages in scalability, availability, and operational simplicity.

Chapter 6

Foundations of SD-WAN Architecture and Deployment

6.1 Introduction

Software-Defined Wide Area Networking (SD-WAN) represents a transformative approach to enterprise network architecture, fundamentally changing how organizations connect distributed sites, cloud resources, and remote users. As businesses increasingly adopt cloud services, SaaS applications, and hybrid work models, traditional WAN architectures built primarily on MPLS connections have become both expensive and inflexible. SD-WAN addresses these challenges by abstracting network hardware from its control mechanism, enabling centralized management, intelligent traffic routing, and the ability to leverage multiple transport technologies simultaneously.

The evolution from traditional WAN to SD-WAN is not merely a technological upgrade – it represents a paradigm shift in network design philosophy. Traditional WANs were built on the assumption that traffic would follow predictable patterns, typically following a hub-and-spoke model where branch offices connected to a central data center. However, the modern enterprise operates in a fundamentally different environment. Applications are increasingly hosted in multiple cloud platforms, users access resources from anywhere, and real-time collaboration tools demand consistent performance regardless of location.

This chapter explores the foundational elements that make SD-WAN possible and effective. We will examine the architectural components that separate SD-WAN from traditional networking approaches, understand how transport layer independence enables flexibility and cost optimization, explore the intelligence that drives application performance, review the various deployment models available to organizations, and investigate the features that ensure network resilience and business continuity.

Understanding these foundations is critical for network architects, engineers, and IT leaders who are evaluating, designing, or implementing SD-WAN solutions. The decisions made at the architectural level will impact performance, security, cost, and operational efficiency for years to come. This chapter provides the technical depth necessary to make informed decisions while maintaining a practical focus on real-world implementation considerations.

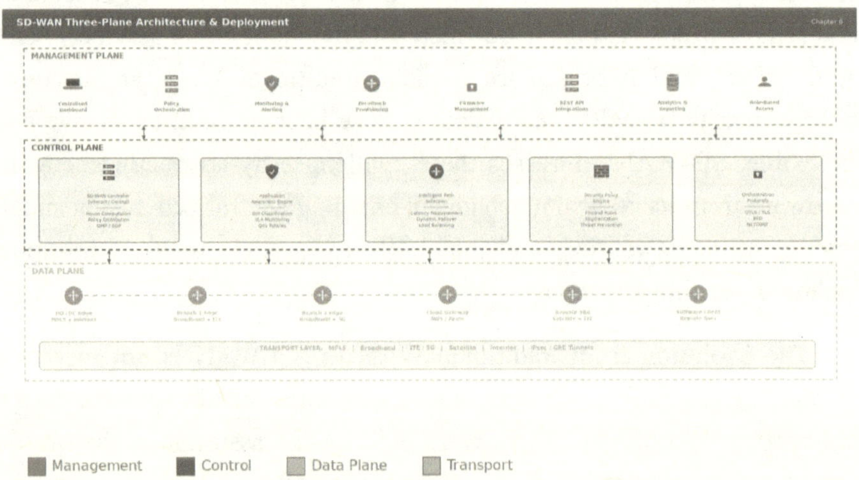

Figure 6.1: SD-WAN Three-Plane Architecture with Transport Independence

6.2 SD-WAN Core Components: The Control Plane, Data Plane, and Management Plane

SD-WAN architecture is built upon three fundamental planes, each serving distinct but interconnected functions. This separation of concerns is central to the software-defined approach and enables the flexibility, scalability, and intelligence that distinguish SD-WAN from traditional WAN technologies.

6.2.1 The Control Plane

The control plane serves as the brain of the SD-WAN architecture, responsible for making decisions about how traffic should be routed across the network. Unlike traditional routing protocols that operate in a distributed fashion with each router making independent decisions, the SD-WAN control plane typically operates in a centralized or hierarchical manner, providing a comprehensive view of the entire WAN environment.

Architecture and Functions

The control plane maintains several critical responsibilities. First, it establishes and maintains secure tunnels between SD-WAN endpoints, whether they are branch offices, data centers, cloud gateways, or remote users. These tunnels form the overlay network that operates independently of the underlying transport infrastructure. The control plane continuously monitors the health and performance characteristics of these tunnels, collecting metrics such as latency, jitter, packet loss, and available bandwidth.

Second, the control plane makes routing decisions based on application requirements, network conditions, and configured policies. When a packet arrives at an SD-WAN edge device, the control plane's policies determine which path that packet should take. These decisions are not static; they adapt in real-time based on current network conditions and application performance requirements.

Third, the control plane distributes policy and configuration information to all SD-WAN devices in the network. When an administrator defines a new policy – such as directing all video conferencing traffic to the highest quality path or ensuring that financial applications receive priority treatment – the control plane propagates this policy to all relevant devices, ensuring consistent behavior across the entire WAN.

Implementation Models

SD-WAN vendors implement the control plane using various architectural models. Some solutions employ a fully centralized controller that maintains complete authority over routing decisions. This approach offers maximum visibility and control but requires that all edge devices maintain connectivity to the central controller. Other implementations use a hierarchical model where regional controllers manage subsets of the network, with a master controller providing overall coordination. This approach can improve scalability and provide better resilience against controller failures.

Some modern SD-WAN platforms have moved toward a distributed control plane model where edge devices share routing information peer-to-peer while still receiving policy guidance from a central orchestrator. This hybrid approach attempts to balance the benefits of centralized policy management with the resilience and reduced latency of distributed decision-making.

Security Considerations

The control plane represents a critical security component. Compromise of the control plane could allow an attacker to redirect traffic, disrupt network connectivity, or gain visibility into network topology and traffic patterns. Therefore, SD-WAN solutions implement multiple security layers for control plane protection. These typically include encrypted control channels using protocols such as TLS or DTLS, strong authentication mechanisms to prevent rogue devices from joining the network, and integrity checking to ensure that policy information has not been tampered with during distribution.

6.2.2 The Data Plane

While the control plane makes decisions, the data plane is responsible for actually forwarding packets across the network. The data plane operates at the SD-WAN edge devices—appliances, virtual machines, or software agents deployed at branch offices, data centers, and other locations where traffic enters or exits the SD-WAN overlay network.

Packet Processing and Forwarding

When a packet arrives at an SD-WAN edge device from the local network, the data plane performs several operations. First, it classifies the packet to determine which application generated it. This classification may be based on simple characteristics like source and destination IP addresses and port numbers, or it may employ more sophisticated techniques such as deep packet inspection (DPI) to identify applications even when they use dynamic ports or encryption.

Once the application is identified, the data plane consults the policies provided by the control plane to determine how this traffic should be handled. Should it be sent over the primary MPLS connection, the backup internet connection, or split across multiple paths? Does it require encryption? Should it receive priority treatment through quality-of-service mechanisms? The data plane applies these policies in real-time to each packet.

The forwarding decision also includes selecting the appropriate tunnel and transport path. In a typical SD-WAN deployment, multiple tunnels may exist between any two sites, each using a different underlying transport (MPLS, broadband internet, LTE). The data plane selects the tunnel that best meets the policy requirements for the specific application while considering current network conditions.

Performance Optimization

Modern SD-WAN data planes incorporate several technologies to optimize performance. Packet deduplication identifies redundant data being transmitted across the WAN and sends it only once, reducing bandwidth consumption. This is particularly effective for backup traffic or when multiple users are accessing similar content.

Forward error correction (FEC) adds redundant data to transmissions, allowing the receiving device to reconstruct packets that are lost in transit without requiring retransmission. This technique is valuable for real-time applications like voice and video where retransmission would introduce unacceptable delay.

Traffic shaping and queuing mechanisms ensure that high-priority traffic receives preferential treatment. The data plane can implement multiple queuing strategies, from simple priority queuing to sophisticated weighted fair queuing algorithms that balance the needs of different applications while preventing starvation of lower-priority traffic.

Data Plane Distribution

The data plane is inherently distributed—each edge device operates its own data plane instance. This distribution is essential for performance, as forwarding decisions must be made with minimal latency. However, it creates challenges for ensuring consistent policy application across all devices. The control plane addresses this challenge through centralized policy distribution and configuration management.

Some SD-WAN architectures implement data plane functions not just at traditional edge appliances but also in cloud gateways, virtual instances within cloud platforms, and even on end-user devices. This extends the SD-WAN fabric to wherever traffic originates or terminates, enabling consistent policy application regardless of location.

6.2.3 The Management Plane

The management plane provides the interface through which administrators interact with the SD-WAN infrastructure. While the control plane handles real-time operational decisions and the data plane forwards traffic, the management plane focuses on configuration, monitoring, troubleshooting, and reporting.

Configuration and Orchestration

The management plane's primary function is configuration management. Through a centralized management interface—typically a web-based dashboard or API—administrators can define network policies, configure security settings, establish routing preferences, and manage device deployment. This centralized approach dramatically simplifies network management compared to traditional WANs where each router required individual configuration.

Modern SD-WAN management platforms support zero-touch provisioning, allowing new edge devices to be shipped directly to remote locations where non-technical staff can simply connect them to power and network. The device automatically contacts the management plane, downloads its configuration, and becomes operational without requiring on-site technical expertise.

Template-based configuration is another key management plane feature. Rather than configuring each site individually, administrators create configuration templates that can be applied to multiple similar sites. Variables within templates accommodate site-specific details like IP addresses and circuit identifiers, while maintaining consistent policies and security settings across all deployments.

Monitoring and Analytics

The management plane collects and presents operational data from across the SD-WAN infrastructure. This includes real-time metrics on application performance, link utilization, user experience, and security events. Advanced SD-WAN platforms employ analytics engines that process this data to identify trends, predict potential issues, and provide recommendations for optimization.

Application-level monitoring provides visibility into how specific applications are performing across the network. Administrators can see metrics like response time, throughput, and availability for critical applications such as Office 365, Salesforce, or custom business applications. This visibility enables proactive problem resolution before users experience significant impact.

Path performance monitoring tracks the health and characteristics of each transport link. The management plane displays metrics such as latency, jitter, packet loss, and available bandwidth for every connection in the network. Historical data allows administrators to identify patterns, such as links that consistently degrade during specific times of day or that are approaching capacity limits.

Troubleshooting and Diagnostics

When issues arise, the management plane provides tools for rapid diagnosis and resolution. Packet capture capabilities allow administrators to capture and analyze traffic flows without physically accessing remote devices. Path testing tools can simulate application traffic to verify that routing policies are working correctly and that adequate performance is available.

Many SD-WAN management platforms incorporate artificial intelligence and machine learning to assist with troubleshooting. These systems can correlate multiple data sources to identify root causes, such as recognizing that poor application performance at multiple sites correlates with a degraded internet connection at a regional data center.

Reporting and Compliance

The management plane generates reports for capacity planning, compliance demonstration, and executive visibility. These reports might include application usage trends, security incident summaries, availability statistics, and cost analysis showing how much bandwidth different applications consume across various transport types.

For organizations with compliance requirements, the management plane can demonstrate policy enforcement, track configuration changes with full audit trails, and provide evidence of security controls.

Role-based access control (RBAC) within the management plane ensures that different administrators have appropriate levels of access, preventing unauthorized changes while enabling operational efficiency.

6.2.4 Integration and Interdependence

While conceptually separate, these three planes work in tight coordination. The management plane configures policies that the control plane interprets and distributes to the data plane for enforcement. The data plane reports performance metrics to the control plane, which uses this information for routing decisions and forwards aggregated data to the management plane for presentation and analysis.

This architecture provides several advantages. The separation of concerns allows each plane to be optimized for its specific function – the data plane for high-speed packet forwarding, the control plane for intelligent decision-making, and the management plane for human interaction and analysis. The centralization of control and management planes enables consistent policy application and simplified operations, while the distribution of the data plane ensures performance and scalability.

6.3 SD-WAN Transport Layer Independence: Leveraging Broadband, LTE, and MPLS

One of SD-WAN's most transformative characteristics is transport layer independence—the ability to utilize any available network connection regardless of the underlying technology or service provider. This capability fundamentally changes the economics and flexibility of WAN connectivity.

6.3.1 The Traditional WAN Transport Paradigm

Traditional enterprise WANs were typically built on MPLS (Multiprotocol Label Switching) connections leased from telecommunications carriers. MPLS offers several valuable characteristics: predictable performance with guaranteed bandwidth and latency, inherent quality of service capabilities, any-to-any connectivity between sites without requiring full mesh configurations, and a degree of security through isolation from the public internet.

However, MPLS connections come with significant limitations. They are expensive, with costs that scale linearly with bandwidth—doubling bandwidth typically doubles cost. Provisioning new MPLS circuits or increasing capacity often requires weeks or months, limiting organizational agility. The hub-and-spoke topology commonly used with MPLS creates inefficiencies in the cloud era, as traffic from a branch office to a cloud application must backhaul through a central data center rather than accessing the cloud directly.

6.3.2 Broadband Internet as WAN Transport

SD-WAN enables organizations to leverage commodity broadband internet connections as WAN transport. Cable, DSL, fiber, and fixed wireless broadband services typically offer substantially higher bandwidth at much lower cost than MPLS circuits. A broadband connection providing 100 Mbps of symmetric bandwidth might cost a fraction of a 10 Mbps MPLS circuit.

Performance Considerations

The primary concern with broadband as WAN transport is the lack of performance guarantees. Internet connections are "best effort" services subject to variable latency, packet loss, and potential congestion. Performance can vary based on time of day, overall internet congestion, routing decisions made by upstream providers, and shared bandwidth with other subscribers.

SD-WAN addresses these concerns through several mechanisms. By continuously monitoring multiple paths and intelligently steering traffic, SD-WAN can work around transient internet performance issues. When latency spikes on one path, traffic can be redirected to alternatives. Forward error correction can compensate for packet loss without requiring retransmission delays. Application-specific policies ensure that critical traffic receives priority treatment even across best-effort transport.

Security Implications

Using internet connections for WAN transport introduces security considerations. Traditional MPLS networks provide some security through isolation—your traffic is separated from other customers' traffic within the carrier's infrastructure. Internet connections lack this isolation; traffic traverses the public internet where it could potentially be intercepted or modified.

SD-WAN compensates by implementing encryption for all traffic traversing internet connections. Most SD-WAN solutions create encrypted tunnels (typically using IPsec or proprietary protocols) between edge devices, ensuring that even though traffic crosses the public internet, it remains confidential and protected from tampering. This encryption is applied transparently, without requiring changes to applications or end-user devices.

Deployment Considerations

When deploying broadband connections for SD-WAN, several practical considerations arise. Circuit diversity is important—using multiple broadband services from different providers helps ensure that a problem affecting one provider doesn't create a single point of failure. Physical diversity matters too; ideally, connections should enter the building through different paths to avoid a single point of failure from construction accidents or natural disasters.

Internet service providers differ in performance characteristics. Some organizations conduct testing before deployment to understand typical latency, jitter, and loss characteristics of different providers in specific locations. This information helps in establishing realistic performance expectations and configuring appropriate policies.

6.3.3 LTE and 5G as WAN Transport

Cellular networks, particularly LTE and emerging 5G services, provide another transport option for SD-WAN. Cellular connections offer unique advantages: they provide connectivity in locations where wired services are unavailable or prohibitively expensive to deploy, they can be activated quickly (often within days), and they provide inherent diversity from wired services.

Use Cases for Cellular Transport

Cellular connections serve several roles in SD-WAN deployments. As primary connectivity, they support temporary locations, construction sites, pop-up retail locations, and sites in areas without adequate wired infrastructure. As backup connectivity, they provide failover capability when primary connections fail, ensuring business continuity. As active-active transport, some organizations use cellular connections in parallel with wired services, with SD-WAN distributing traffic across all available paths.

Certain industries particularly benefit from cellular SD-WAN transport. Retail organizations use LTE to quickly establish connectivity for new store locations or seasonal pop-ups. Financial services use cellular connections as out-of-band backup to ensure ATM availability even when primary connections fail. Transportation and logistics companies use cellular connectivity for vehicles and mobile assets.

Performance Characteristics

Cellular networks exhibit different performance characteristics than wired connections. Latency tends to be higher and more variable, particularly during mobility or under congestion. Bandwidth can vary significantly based on signal strength, network congestion, and the number of nearby users sharing the same cell tower. Data caps are common, with some cellular plans charging substantial overage fees when usage exceeds monthly allowances.

SD-WAN helps manage these characteristics through intelligent traffic steering. When cellular connections serve as backup, SD-WAN can ensure they're only used when primary connections fail, managing data consumption. When used as active transport, SD-WAN can direct only latency-tolerant or non-critical applications over cellular while reserving latency-sensitive traffic for wired connections. Usage monitoring within the SD-WAN management plane provides visibility into data consumption, helping organizations avoid unexpected overage charges.

Deployment Models

Organizations deploy cellular SD-WAN transport in various configurations. Integrated SD-WAN appliances with built-in cellular modems provide a clean, single-vendor solution. External cellular routers can connect to standard SD-WAN appliances, offering flexibility in choosing cellular providers and upgrading cellular technology independently. Cloud-based SD-WAN implementations might connect directly to cellular devices without requiring on-premises hardware.

Some SD-WAN solutions support SIM management capabilities, allowing centralized control over cellular subscriptions, automatic carrier switching in multi-carrier deployments, and remote troubleshooting of cellular connectivity issues.

6.3.4 MPLS in the SD-WAN Era

Despite SD-WAN's ability to leverage alternative transports, MPLS remains relevant for many organizations. MPLS provides predictable performance that may be essential for certain applications, particularly those with strict latency and jitter requirements like voice communications or real-time financial trading systems. Some organizations operate in regions where reliable broadband or cellular services are unavailable, making MPLS the only viable option. Regulatory or compliance requirements may mandate the use of private, isolated networks that MPLS provides.

Hybrid Approaches

Most SD-WAN deployments adopt a hybrid approach, combining MPLS with broadband and sometimes cellular connections. This approach maximizes both performance and cost efficiency. Critical applications use MPLS for guaranteed performance, while less-sensitive traffic uses lower-cost internet connections. As broadband connections prove reliable, organizations can gradually reduce MPLS bandwidth (and costs) while maintaining the circuits for applications that specifically require them.

SD-WAN excels at managing hybrid transport environments. A single SD-WAN platform can simultaneously manage MPLS circuits, multiple internet connections, and cellular backup, applying appropriate policies to each based on application requirements, current performance, and cost considerations.

6.3.5 Transport Bonding and Aggregation

Some SD-WAN solutions implement transport bonding, combining multiple connections to appear as a single logical link with aggregated bandwidth. When transmitting large files or bulk data, the SD-WAN system can split traffic across multiple circuits, effectively adding their bandwidth together. For example, bonding two 50 Mbps broadband connections could provide near 100 Mbps throughput for large transfers.

Bonding works best for elastic applications that can tolerate some packet reordering. Real-time applications like voice and video typically don't benefit from bonding since their traffic must arrive in order, but backup operations, file transfers, and bulk data replication can see substantial performance improvements.

6.4 Intelligent Path Selection and Application Steering: Optimizing Performance and User Experience

The intelligence embedded within SD-WAN systems to select optimal paths and steer applications differentiates it from simple load balancing or basic routing protocols. This intelligence operates continuously, making microsecond decisions about how to handle each packet while adapting to changing network conditions and application requirements.

Application Identification and Classification

Before intelligent path selection can occur, the SD-WAN system must identify what application generated each packet. Application identification employs multiple techniques working in concert.

Port-Based Classification

The simplest method examines TCP or UDP port numbers. Many applications use standard ports—HTTP on port 80, HTTPS on port 443, SSH on port 22. While straightforward, this method has limitations. Many modern applications use non-standard ports, multiple applications may share common ports (particularly 80 and 443), and applications increasingly use dynamic port allocation where the port varies between sessions.

Deep Packet Inspection (DPI)

DPI examines packet payloads to identify application signatures—patterns in the data that uniquely identify specific applications. Even when applications use standard ports like 443, DPI can distinguish between Office 365, Salesforce, and other SaaS applications based on characteristics of their encrypted handshakes, certificate information, and traffic patterns.

Modern DPI engines maintain databases of thousands of application signatures, regularly updated as new applications emerge and existing applications evolve. The inspection occurs at line rate without significantly impacting performance, using optimized algorithms and hardware acceleration where available.

Heuristic and Behavioral Analysis

Some applications defy signature-based identification, particularly new or custom applications. Advanced SD-WAN systems employ behavioral analysis, examining characteristics like traffic patterns, packet sizes, timing relationships between packets, and communication endpoints to infer the application type. Machine learning models can be trained to recognize application behaviors, improving accuracy over time.

Context-Aware Classification

The most sophisticated systems incorporate contextual information into classification. Which user generated the traffic? What device are they using? What is the business priority of their role? Context-aware classification allows the same application to be treated differently based on who is using it—a video conference for a sales call with a customer might receive priority over a recreational video stream.

Path Performance Measurement

Intelligent path selection requires real-time knowledge of path characteristics. SD-WAN systems continuously monitor all available paths between sites, measuring multiple performance metrics.

Active Measurement

Active measurement sends synthetic probe packets across paths to measure their characteristics. Probes might be simple ICMP echo requests (pings) or synthetic application traffic designed to mimic real user data. By measuring probe round-trip times, the system calculates latency. Variations in successive probe measurements reveal jitter. Missing probes indicate packet loss.

Active measurement provides real-time visibility into path performance even when no actual user traffic is flowing. This ensures that when traffic needs to use a path, current performance information is available. However, probe traffic consumes bandwidth and may not perfectly represent how the path will perform under load with actual application traffic.

Passive Measurement

Passive measurement observes actual user traffic traversing paths and derives performance metrics from this observation. By tracking acknowledgment packets, the system can calculate round-trip times. Lost packets requiring retransmission indicate path problems. Passive measurement reflects real performance under actual load conditions but only provides data when traffic is actively using a path.

Advanced SD-WAN systems combine active and passive measurement, using probes to maintain baseline visibility while refining estimates based on actual traffic performance.

Bandwidth Measurement

Understanding available bandwidth on each path is crucial for intelligent routing. SD-WAN systems employ several techniques to estimate bandwidth. Some send increasingly large bursts of probe traffic until packet loss occurs, indicating the path's capacity limit. Others observe how quickly the path can transmit actual application traffic. Historical data helps identify typical bandwidth availability and patterns of variation.

Path Scoring

Rather than treating measurement metrics independently, SD-WAN systems typically combine multiple metrics into composite path scores. A path might be fast but lossy, or slow but reliable. The scoring system weighs different metrics based on application requirements—latency matters most for interactive applications, while loss matters more for bulk transfers.

Application-Aware Routing

With applications identified and paths characterized, the SD-WAN system can make intelligent routing decisions matching application requirements to path capabilities.

Policy-Based Steering

Administrators define policies that specify requirements for different application classes. A policy might state: "Voice traffic requires less than 150ms latency, less than 30ms jitter, and less than 1% packet loss. Prefer MPLS, but use broadband if MPLS becomes unavailable or doesn't meet requirements." When the SD-WAN system identifies voice traffic, it evaluates all available paths against these requirements and selects the best match.

Policies can be remarkably sophisticated. They might specify different requirements for different times of day, treat traffic differently based on source or destination, or implement complex decision trees considering multiple factors. Some systems support policies based on business metrics like the cost of using different paths or contractual obligations with service providers.

Dynamic Path Selection

Path selection isn't static—it adapts continuously as conditions change. If the currently used path begins to degrade, the SD-WAN system can redirect traffic to an alternative path without disrupting existing connections. This adaptability provides resilience against transient network problems that would severely impact performance in traditional networks.

The switch to alternative paths must be implemented carefully to avoid oscillation, where traffic constantly shifts between paths in response to minor fluctuations. SD-WAN systems employ dampening algorithms that require persistent condition changes before switching paths, and hysteresis that requires conditions to improve significantly before switching back to a previously problematic path.

Per-Packet vs. Per-Flow Routing

SD-WAN systems must decide at what granularity to make routing decisions. Per-flow routing assigns all packets belonging to the same session (defined by source/destination addresses and ports) to the same path. This approach prevents packet reordering, which can confuse some applications and reduce TCP performance. However, it means that once a flow starts, it continues on its initial path even if better paths become available.

Per-packet routing can send different packets of the same flow over different paths, enabling fine-grained load distribution and rapid response to path changes. However, it requires sophisticated packet reordering at the receiving end to prevent application problems. Some SD-WAN systems use hybrid approaches, employing per-flow routing for latency-sensitive applications while using per-packet routing for bulk transfers where reordering is less problematic.

Quality of Service (QoS) Integration

Path selection works in concert with QoS mechanisms to optimize application performance. Even with optimal path selection, if too much traffic converges on a path, congestion will occur and performance will suffer. QoS provides the tools to prioritize important traffic when congestion arises.

Traffic Classification for QoS

The application identification performed for path selection also serves QoS. Once an application is identified, it can be assigned to a QoS class with associated priority level. Critical business applications might receive "expedited forwarding" treatment, ensuring minimal delay even during congestion. Bulk transfer applications might receive "best effort" treatment, using available bandwidth without preventing higher-priority traffic from flowing smoothly.

Queuing and Scheduling

SD-WAN devices implement multiple queuing mechanisms. Priority queuing ensures that high-priority traffic is transmitted before lower-priority traffic. Weighted fair queuing allocates bandwidth proportionally, giving more to high-priority traffic while ensuring that lower-priority traffic isn't completely starved. Deficit round-robin queuing provides fairness while maintaining efficiency.

The choice of queuing mechanism affects how traffic behaves under congestion. The SD-WAN system must balance the need to prioritize critical applications against the need to fairly serve all legitimate traffic and avoid pathological behaviors where certain flows consume all available bandwidth.

End-to-End QoS

QoS within the SD-WAN overlay is only part of the picture. For true end-to-end quality of service, QoS markings must be honored by the underlying transport networks. SD-WAN systems can mark packets (using DSCP fields in IP headers) to request specific handling from carrier networks. However, not all carriers honor these markings, and internet traffic typically receives best-effort treatment regardless of markings.

For MPLS connections, coordinating QoS between the SD-WAN overlay and the MPLS underlay is important. The SD-WAN system should map its QoS classes to the QoS classes supported by the MPLS provider, ensuring consistent treatment throughout the packet's journey.

User Experience Monitoring and Optimization

The ultimate goal of intelligent path selection and application steering is optimal user experience. Advanced SD-WAN systems go beyond simple network metrics to measure actual user experience.

Application Performance Monitoring

Rather than just measuring network latency, packet loss, and bandwidth, sophisticated systems measure application-specific metrics. For web applications, this includes page load time, time to first byte, and transaction completion rates. For voice applications, it includes Mean Opinion Score (MOS), a perceptual quality metric. For video, it includes buffering frequency and resolution delivered.

By monitoring these application-level metrics, the SD-WAN system can optimize based on what users actually experience rather than relying solely on network-level proxies. This approach better aligns technical optimization with business objectives.

Synthetic Testing

Some SD-WAN platforms support synthetic testing, where automated agents simulate user interactions with applications. These synthetic transactions provide proactive visibility into application performance, potentially identifying issues before users report problems. Synthetic testing also enables performance baselining and benchmarking, helping organizations understand whether performance changes result from network issues, application issues, or normal variation.

Continuous Optimization

The best SD-WAN systems don't simply apply static policies—they continuously learn and optimize. Machine learning models can identify patterns in application behavior and network performance, predicting when degradation is likely to occur and proactively adjusting routing. Anomaly detection alerts administrators to unusual patterns that might indicate problems, attacks, or opportunities for optimization.

6.5 SD-WAN Deployment Models: On-Premises, Cloud-Hosted, and Managed Services

Organizations can deploy SD-WAN using various models, each with distinct characteristics, benefits, and trade-offs. The choice of deployment model significantly impacts implementation complexity, operational responsibility, cost structure, and the extent of control the organization retains.

On-Premises Deployment

In an on-premises deployment, the organization owns or leases all SD-WAN hardware and hosts all software components (control plane, management plane, and data plane) within its own facilities.

Architecture and Components

A typical on-premises deployment includes SD-WAN appliances at each branch office and data center. These might be purpose-built hardware devices optimized for packet processing and encryption, or general-purpose servers running SD-WAN software. The control plane and management plane typically run in the organization's data center, either on dedicated servers or within the existing virtualization infrastructure.

Organizations must also implement high availability for centralized components. This usually involves deploying redundant controllers in different data centers or availability zones, with automatic failover if the primary controller fails. Geographic distribution of controllers improves resilience and can reduce latency for distant sites.

Benefits of On-Premises Deployment

Complete control represents the primary advantage of on-premises deployment. The organization controls all aspects of the SD-WAN infrastructure—when upgrades occur, what features are enabled, how data is handled, and how systems are configured. For organizations with strict compliance requirements or concerns about data sovereignty, on-premises deployment ensures that all management data and logs remain within the organization's control.

Performance optimization is possible through careful tuning and integration with other on-premises systems. The SD-WAN infrastructure can be tightly integrated with existing network management tools, security systems, and orchestration platforms. Custom integrations and automation workflows can be developed to meet specific organizational needs.

For very large deployments with hundreds or thousands of sites, on-premises deployment may offer cost advantages over recurring managed service fees. The capital expenditure for hardware and licenses may be lower over time than cumulative service fees, though this calculation depends on numerous factors including organizational scale, negotiated pricing, and the cost of internal IT resources.

Challenges and Considerations

On-premises deployment requires substantial technical expertise. The organization must have staff capable of designing, implementing, and operating the SD-WAN infrastructure. This includes understanding networking, security, the specific SD-WAN platform, and integration with other systems. Staffing requirements extend beyond initial deployment to ongoing operations, troubleshooting, and optimization.

The organization bears responsibility for all infrastructure maintenance. Hardware must be maintained, repaired, or replaced when it fails. Software must be patched and upgraded, which requires testing to ensure compatibility and smooth operation. High availability and disaster recovery are the organization's responsibility, requiring careful design and regular testing.

Capital expenditure can be significant. While operational costs may be lower over time, the initial investment in hardware, software licenses, and implementation services can be substantial. Budget approval for large capital expenditures may be more difficult to obtain than approval for operational expenditures spread over time.

Cloud-Hosted Deployment

Cloud-hosted SD-WAN deployments place the control plane and management plane in a cloud provider's infrastructure (such as AWS, Azure, or Google Cloud Platform), while edge devices at branch offices connect to these cloud-hosted components.

Architecture and Components

In a cloud-hosted model, the vendor or organization deploys SD-WAN controllers and management systems as virtual machines or containers in cloud infrastructure. These components run in the cloud provider's data centers, benefiting from the cloud's infrastructure, geographic distribution, and resilience features.

Edge devices at branch offices remain on-premises but are typically lightweight, since heavy processing can be offloaded to the cloud. Some cloud-hosted deployments use virtual SD-WAN appliances within cloud environments to extend the SD-WAN fabric to cloud-based resources, enabling seamless connectivity between branches, data centers, and cloud applications.

Chapter 7

The Cybersecurity Baseline: Threats and Trust Models

7.1 Introduction

The modern enterprise network operates in an environment of persistent threat. As organizations migrate to cloud infrastructure, embrace remote work, and connect an expanding array of devices and services, the traditional security perimeter has dissolved. What once was a clearly defined boundary between trusted internal networks and untrusted external threats has evolved into a complex mesh of connections, each representing potential vulnerability.

This chapter examines the fundamental cybersecurity challenges facing contemporary networks and introduces the architectural principles required to address them. We begin with a comprehensive analysis of the threat landscape, exploring the attack vectors and methodologies that adversaries employ. From there, we trace the evolution of network security architectures, examining how defensive strategies have adapted to increasingly sophisticated threats. Finally, we explore Zero Trust Network Access (ZTNA) as a paradigm shift in security thinking, along with the practical implementations of micro-segmentation, least privilege access, and compliance-driven network design.

Understanding these concepts is essential for any network professional, security architect, or IT leader responsible for protecting organizational assets in the digital age. The transition from perimeter-based security to identity-centric, context-aware access control represents one of the most significant shifts in cybersecurity philosophy in decades.

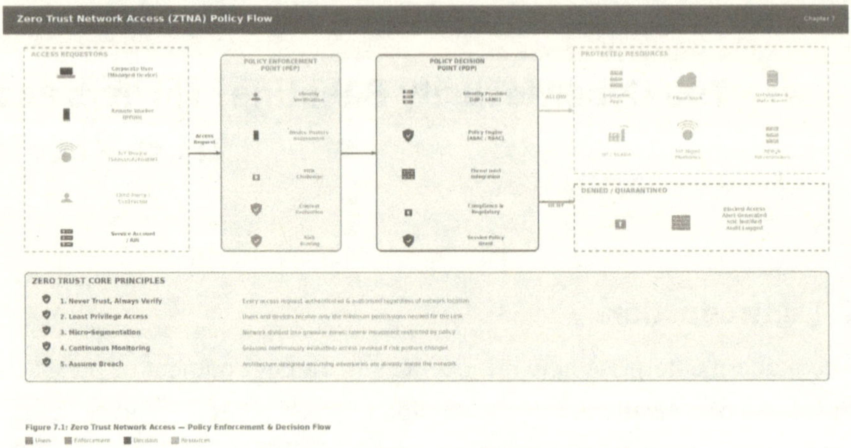

Figure 7.1: Zero Trust Network Access — Policy Enforcement & Decision Flow

7.2 Comprehensive Threat Landscape Analysis

The Nature of Modern Cyber Threats

The threat landscape facing modern organizations is characterized by increasing sophistication, automation, and specialization. Attack campaigns are no longer the domain of isolated hackers working in isolation. Today's adversaries range from state-sponsored advanced persistent threat (APT) groups to organized criminal syndicates, from automated botnet operators to insider threats within organizations themselves.

The motivations driving these threats are equally diverse. Financial gain remains a primary driver, with ransomware attacks generating billions of dollars annually for criminal organizations. Espionage, both corporate and state-sponsored, seeks to steal intellectual property, trade secrets, and sensitive government information. Hacktivism pursues ideological or political goals through network disruption and data exposure. Understanding these motivations helps security professionals anticipate attack patterns and prioritize defensive measures.

Malware: The Persistent Threat

Malware, or malicious software, encompasses any code designed to damage systems, steal data, or gain unauthorized access. The malware ecosystem has evolved dramatically over the past two decades, from simple viruses that replicated themselves to sophisticated, modular frameworks that adapt to their environment.

Viruses and Worms

Traditional viruses attach themselves to legitimate programs and spread when users execute infected files. Worms, by contrast, self-propagate across networks without human intervention. The 2017 WannaCry ransomware worm demonstrated the devastating potential of self-spreading malware, exploiting the EternalBlue vulnerability to infect hundreds of thousands of systems across 150 countries in a matter of hours.

Trojans and Remote Access Tools

Trojan horses disguise themselves as legitimate software while performing malicious actions in the background. Modern trojans often function as remote access tools (RATs), providing attackers with persistent backdoor access to compromised systems. These tools enable keystroke logging, screen capture, file exfiltration, and lateral movement within networks.

Ransomware

Ransomware has emerged as one of the most economically damaging forms of malware. These programs encrypt victim data and demand payment for decryption keys. Modern ransomware operations often employ double extortion tactics, threatening to publish stolen data if ransom demands are not met. The evolution of ransomware-as-a-service

(RaaS) has lowered barriers to entry, enabling less sophisticated criminals to launch devastating attacks.

Advanced Persistent Threats (APTs)

APT campaigns represent the apex of malware sophistication. Typically associated with nation-state actors, APTs employ custom-developed tools, zero-day exploits, and carefully planned multi-stage attacks designed to maintain long-term, undetected access to target networks. APT groups often spend months or years inside compromised networks, slowly expanding access and extracting sensitive information.

Malware Defense Strategies

Defending against malware requires layered security controls. Endpoint protection platforms combine signature-based detection, behavioral analysis, and machine learning to identify and block malicious code. Regular patching eliminates known vulnerabilities that malware exploits. Application whitelisting restricts execution to approved software, preventing unauthorized programs from running. Security awareness training reduces the likelihood of users inadvertently executing malicious files.

Distributed Denial of Service (DDoS) Attacks

DDoS attacks seek to overwhelm systems, networks, or applications with traffic, rendering them unavailable to legitimate users. These attacks have grown dramatically in scale, with some reaching terabits per second in traffic volume.

Volumetric Attacks

Volumetric DDoS attacks flood targets with massive amounts of traffic, consuming available bandwidth and overwhelming network infrastructure. Amplification attacks leverage protocols like DNS, NTP, and SSDP to multiply attack traffic, allowing relatively small botnets to generate enormous traffic volumes. The 2016 Dyn attack, which disrupted major websites including Twitter, Netflix, and Reddit, demonstrated the internet-wide impact possible from large-scale DDoS campaigns.

Protocol Attacks

Protocol attacks exploit weaknesses in network protocols to exhaust server resources. SYN flood attacks, for example, send numerous TCP connection requests without completing the handshake, filling connection tables and preventing legitimate connections. These attacks target the network and transport layers of the OSI model.

Application Layer Attacks

Application layer DDoS attacks target web applications with seemingly legitimate requests designed to exhaust server resources. These attacks are often more difficult to detect and mitigate than volumetric attacks because they mimic normal user behavior. A small number of attackers can sometimes generate enough resource-intensive requests to bring down poorly optimized applications.

DDoS Mitigation Strategies

Effective DDoS mitigation combines multiple approaches. Content delivery networks (CDNs) and cloud-based scrubbing services can absorb and filter attack traffic before it reaches origin servers. Rate limiting restricts the number of requests from individual sources. Anycast routing distributes traffic across multiple data centers, making it more difficult for attackers to overwhelm any single location. Redundant infrastructure ensures service availability even during attacks.

Phishing and Social Engineering

While technical controls protect against many automated threats, human psychology remains a critical vulnerability. Phishing attacks exploit human trust and cognitive biases to trick users into divulging credentials, executing malware, or authorizing fraudulent transactions.

Email Phishing

Traditional phishing campaigns send mass emails impersonating trusted organizations, directing recipients to fake websites designed to capture credentials or deliver malware. Despite widespread awareness, phishing remains highly effective. Modern phishing kits enable attackers to clone legitimate websites rapidly and deploy convincing campaigns with minimal technical expertise.

Spear Phishing and Whaling

Spear phishing targets specific individuals with personalized messages based on reconnaissance. Attackers research their targets through social media, corporate websites, and other public sources to craft convincing pretexts. Whaling attacks specifically target high-value individuals like executives and administrators who possess privileged access.

Smishing and Vishing

As organizations have implemented better email security controls, attackers have turned to SMS phishing (smishing) and voice phishing (vishing). These attacks leverage the trusted nature of phone communications and users' lower security awareness on mobile devices.

Business Email Compromise (BEC)

BEC attacks represent a particularly damaging form of social engineering. Attackers compromise or impersonate executive email accounts to authorize fraudulent wire transfers or redirect payroll deposits. The FBI estimates BEC attacks have cost organizations over $40 billion globally.

Social Engineering Defense

Defending against social engineering requires a combination of technical controls and human factors. Email filtering and authentication protocols like SPF, DKIM, and DMARC reduce phishing email delivery. Multi-factor authentication ensures that compromised credentials alone cannot grant access. Security awareness training teaches users to recognize and report suspicious communications. Establishing verification procedures for sensitive transactions creates additional checkpoints that can catch fraud attempts.

Man-in-the-Middle (MitM) Attacks

MitM attacks occur when an adversary intercepts communications between two parties, potentially reading, modifying, or injecting data without the knowledge of either party. These attacks threaten the confidentiality and integrity of data in transit.

Network-Level MitM

On local networks, attackers can use ARP spoofing to redirect traffic through their systems before forwarding it to intended destinations. This technique is particularly effective on public WiFi networks and other shared network segments. DNS spoofing redirects users to malicious sites by corrupting DNS responses.

SSL/TLS Interception

Some MitM attacks target encrypted connections by presenting fraudulent SSL/TLS certificates. If users ignore certificate warnings or if attackers have compromised certificate authorities, they can decrypt, inspect, and potentially modify even encrypted traffic.

Session Hijacking

Session hijacking attacks steal or predict session tokens to impersonate authenticated users. Once attackers obtain valid session credentials, they can access protected resources as if they were the legitimate user.

MitM Prevention

Strong encryption protocols protect data in transit from interception. Certificate pinning ensures applications only accept specific certificates, preventing fraudulent certificate attacks. VPNs create encrypted tunnels that protect traffic on untrusted networks. HTTPS Strict Transport Security

(HSTS) forces browsers to use encrypted connections. Regular security audits identify vulnerable network configurations that could enable MitM attacks.

Emerging Threats

The threat landscape continues evolving as technology advances. Supply chain attacks compromise software during development or distribution, affecting all downstream users. Cryptojacking malware mines cryptocurrency using victim computing resources. API attacks target the interfaces that connect cloud services and applications. As artificial intelligence becomes more prevalent, adversaries are beginning to explore attacks against machine learning systems through data poisoning and adversarial inputs.

7.3 Evolution of Network Security Architectures

The Castle-and-Moat Model

Traditional network security architectures operated on a simple premise: establish a strong perimeter around trusted internal networks, controlling all traffic entering or leaving through a small number of carefully monitored gateways. This "castle-and-moat" approach assumed that threats existed primarily outside the organizational boundary, while internal networks could be trusted.

This model worked reasonably well when networks were physically contained within corporate facilities, applications ran on-premises, and users accessed resources from office workstations. Security teams focused their resources on perimeter defenses, investing heavily in firewalls, gateway antivirus, and intrusion detection systems positioned at network boundaries.

However, the castle-and-moat model contained inherent weaknesses that would become increasingly problematic. Once attackers breached the perimeter, they often found minimal security controls within internal networks, enabling rapid lateral movement. The model struggled to protect against insider threats and failed to adapt to remote access requirements. As business needs drove network complexity, the clear perimeter began to dissolve.

Firewalls: The First Line of Defense

Firewalls represent one of the oldest and most fundamental network security controls. A firewall examines network traffic against a defined rule set, permitting or blocking traffic based on specified criteria.

Packet Filtering Firewalls

First-generation packet filtering firewalls operate at the network layer, making decisions based on IP addresses, ports, and protocols. These stateless firewalls evaluate each packet independently, without considering the broader context of network sessions. While fast and efficient, packet filtering firewalls provide limited security against sophisticated attacks.

Stateful Inspection Firewalls

Stateful firewalls track the state of network connections, understanding which packets belong to established sessions. This enables them to block unsolicited inbound traffic while permitting response traffic for connections initiated from inside the network. Stateful inspection provided significant security improvements over simple packet filtering and became the standard for enterprise firewalls throughout the 1990s and early 2000s.

Application Layer Firewalls

Next-generation firewalls (NGFWs) operate at the application layer, inspecting the content of network traffic rather than just headers. These devices can identify specific applications regardless of the ports or protocols used, enabling more granular policy enforcement. NGFWs often integrate additional security functions like intrusion prevention, malware scanning, and SSL inspection.

Web Application Firewalls (WAFs)

WAFs specifically protect web applications from attacks like SQL injection, cross-site scripting, and other OWASP Top 10 vulnerabilities. By understanding HTTP/HTTPS protocols and application logic, WAFs can block malicious requests while allowing legitimate traffic to reach web servers.

Firewall Limitations

While essential, firewalls have significant limitations. They cannot decrypt and inspect encrypted traffic without SSL/TLS interception, which introduces its own security and privacy concerns. Firewalls struggle with insider threats since they primarily focus on perimeter security. Modern applications using dynamic ports and encrypted tunnels can evade traditional firewall controls. Perhaps most critically, firewalls cannot protect against threats that originate inside the network perimeter.

Intrusion Detection and Prevention Systems

As attackers developed techniques to evade firewalls, organizations deployed intrusion detection systems (IDS) and intrusion prevention systems (IPS) to provide additional layers of security.

Intrusion Detection Systems (IDS)

IDS devices monitor network traffic for suspicious patterns that might indicate attacks. Signature-based IDS compare traffic against known attack patterns, while anomaly-based IDS establish baselines of normal behavior and alert on deviations. Network-based IDS (NIDS) monitor traffic at strategic points throughout the network, while host-based IDS (HIDS) monitor individual systems for file changes, log anomalies, and suspicious process behavior.

IDS operate passively, generating alerts for security teams to investigate. This approach ensures that false positives don't disrupt legitimate traffic, but it means that attacks continue unimpeded until humans respond to alerts.

Intrusion Prevention Systems (IPS)

IPS devices add active blocking capabilities to intrusion detection. When IPS detect suspicious traffic, they can automatically block the offending traffic, reset connections, or modify packets to remove malicious content. By operating inline with network traffic, IPS can prevent attacks in real-time without waiting for human intervention.

The challenge with IPS deployment is balancing security and availability. Aggressive IPS configurations risk blocking legitimate traffic, potentially disrupting business operations. Conservative configurations may allow attacks to proceed. Tuning IPS to minimize false positives while maintaining effective threat detection requires ongoing effort and expertise.

Modern IDS/IPS Capabilities

Contemporary IDS/IPS platforms incorporate advanced capabilities like SSL decryption, behavioral analysis, threat intelligence integration, and machine learning-based detection. Some systems can identify encrypted malware through analysis of traffic metadata and certificate characteristics, even without decrypting traffic. Integration with security information and event management (SIEM) systems enables correlation of IDS/IPS alerts with data from other security tools.

Virtual Private Networks (VPNs)

As organizations embraced remote work and needed to connect distributed offices, VPNs emerged as the standard solution for secure remote access.

Site-to-Site VPNs

Site-to-site VPNs create encrypted tunnels between networks, enabling organizations to securely connect branch offices to headquarters or to link on-premises infrastructure with cloud resources. These permanent connections typically use IPsec protocols to ensure confidentiality and integrity of data in transit.

Remote Access VPNs

Remote access VPNs allow individual users to connect securely to organizational networks from external locations. When a user establishes a VPN connection, their device receives an internal IP address and can access network resources as if physically present in the office. SSL/TLS VPNs operate through web browsers without requiring dedicated client software, while IPsec VPNs provide more robust security but require client installation.

VPN Limitations and Challenges

Traditional VPNs present several challenges in modern environments. Once authenticated, VPN users typically receive broad network access, creating security risks if their devices are compromised. VPNs can introduce performance bottlenecks as all traffic routes through VPN concentrators. Split tunneling, which routes only corporate traffic through the VPN while allowing direct internet access for other traffic, improves performance but introduces security risks. VPNs also struggle to provide granular access control and lack the contextual awareness needed for risk-based authentication.

The Demilitarized Zone (DMZ)

To reduce exposure of internal networks while hosting internet-facing services, organizations implemented DMZ architectures. A DMZ places public servers in a semi-trusted network zone between the internal network and the internet. Firewalls control traffic between the internet and DMZ, and between the DMZ and internal network.

This segmentation limits the impact of compromised public servers. Attackers who breach a web server in the DMZ still face additional security controls before accessing internal resources. However, DMZ architectures add complexity to network management and require careful rule configuration to function correctly.

Defense in Depth

The evolution of threats drove security professionals toward defense-in-depth strategies, implementing multiple layers of security controls. Rather than relying on a single defensive perimeter, organizations deployed firewalls, IDS/IPS, antivirus, access controls, encryption, security monitoring, and incident response capabilities.

Defense in depth recognizes that no single control is perfect. Layered defenses ensure that if attackers bypass one control, additional security measures can detect and block the attack. This approach also addresses diverse threat vectors, protecting against both external attacks and insider threats.

Network Segmentation

As internal threats became more prominent, organizations began implementing network segmentation to limit lateral movement. Rather than treating the entire internal network as equally trusted, segmentation divides networks into zones based on security requirements and trust levels.

VLANs provide logical segmentation at the data link layer. Access control lists and firewalls enforce policies between segments. Critical systems like database servers, domain controllers, and financial systems reside in restricted segments with limited access. Production networks are separated from development and testing environments.

Effective segmentation reduces the blast radius of security incidents. Ransomware spreading through a flat network can encrypt every accessible system, while properly segmented networks contain the damage to affected segments.

7.4 The Principle of Zero Trust Network Access (ZTNA)

Origins of Zero Trust

The Zero Trust security model emerged from the recognition that traditional perimeter-based security was increasingly inadequate. In 2010, Forrester Research analyst John Kindervag formally introduced the term "Zero Trust" to describe a security model that eliminates the concept of implicit trust based on network location.

Zero Trust challenges the fundamental assumption underlying castle-and-moat security: the idea that internal networks can be trusted. Instead, Zero Trust operates on the principle of "never trust, always verify." No user, device, application, or network segment is inherently trusted simply because of its location or previous verification.

This paradigm shift reflects the reality of modern computing environments. With cloud adoption, mobile devices, IoT, and remote work, the traditional network perimeter has dissolved. Applications and data reside across multiple clouds and on-premises systems. Users access resources from diverse locations and devices. The old model of establishing trust once at the perimeter and then allowing free movement inside the network no longer aligns with architectural reality or security requirements.

Core Principles of Zero Trust

Never Trust, Always Verify

Zero Trust requires continuous verification of every access request, regardless of origin. Authentication happens not just once during network connection, but repeatedly as users access different resources throughout their session. Each request is evaluated independently based on current context and risk factors.

Assume Breach

Zero Trust architecture assumes that breaches have already occurred or will occur. Rather than focusing solely on prevention, Zero Trust emphasizes limiting the impact of inevitable security incidents. This mindset drives security controls toward containment, monitoring, and rapid detection rather than relying exclusively on preventive measures.

Verify Explicitly

Authentication and authorization decisions must consider all available data points: user identity, device health, location, application being accessed, time of day, data sensitivity, and behavior patterns. Context-aware access control replaces simple credential-based authentication.

Apply Least Privilege Access

Users and systems receive only the minimum access required to perform their specific functions. Broad network access is replaced by granular, resource-specific permissions. Just-in-time access grants temporary privileges for specific tasks, automatically revoking them when no longer needed.

Segment and Micro-segment

Zero Trust architectures implement pervasive segmentation, treating every resource as internet-facing and requiring authentication for access. Micro-segmentation creates granular security boundaries around individual workloads, preventing lateral movement even within data centers.

Identity as the New Perimeter

In Zero Trust architecture, identity becomes the primary security perimeter. Rather than securing a network boundary, Zero Trust secures access to individual resources based on verified identity and contextual factors.

Strong Authentication

Zero Trust requires strong authentication mechanisms. Multi-factor authentication (MFA) combines something you know (password), something you have (security token or mobile device), and potentially something you are (biometrics). Passwordless authentication using FIDO2 security keys or biometrics eliminates password-based attacks entirely.

Continuous Authentication

Beyond initial login, Zero Trust systems continuously verify users throughout their sessions. Behavioral biometrics monitor typing patterns, mouse movements, and device handling to detect account takeover attempts. If a session exhibits suspicious behavior—like impossible travel scenarios or unusual access patterns—the system can require re-authentication or terminate the session.

Device Trust and Posture Assessment

User identity alone is insufficient; the security posture of devices must also be verified. Zero Trust systems evaluate whether devices are managed by the organization, have current security patches, run approved software, and have endpoint protection enabled. Devices failing security checks receive restricted access or are blocked entirely.

Network Transformation for Zero Trust

Implementing Zero Trust requires fundamental changes to network architecture.

Software-Defined Perimeter (SDP)

SDP creates one-to-one network connections between users and resources, replacing broad network access. Before establishing connections, SDP authenticates users and verifies device posture. Only after successful authentication does SDP reveal the existence of protected resources and establish encrypted tunnels. This "dark cloud" approach makes infrastructure invisible to unauthorized parties, eliminating reconnaissance opportunities.

Identity-Aware Proxies

Zero Trust access typically routes through identity-aware proxies that authenticate users, verify authorization, and enforce security policies before forwarding requests to protected resources. These proxies can decrypt SSL/TLS traffic for inspection, inject authentication credentials, and log all access for auditing.

Cloud Access Security Brokers (CASB)

CASBs extend Zero Trust principles to cloud applications. Positioned between users and cloud service providers, CASBs enforce security policies, detect unusual behavior, prevent data exfiltration, and provide visibility into cloud usage. CASBs can operate inline (proxying traffic) or out-of-band (monitoring via API integration).

Implementing Zero Trust: Practical Considerations

Phased Adoption

Organizations rarely transition to Zero Trust overnight. Most implementations follow phased approaches, beginning with high-value resources, remote access, or new projects. Early wins build organizational support and provide learning opportunities before expanding Zero Trust to all resources.

Integration with Existing Infrastructure

Zero Trust must coexist with legacy systems during transition periods. Modern Zero Trust platforms integrate with existing identity providers, security tools, and applications. APIs and standards like SAML, OAuth, and OIDC enable interoperability.

User Experience

Poorly implemented Zero Trust can frustrate users with excessive authentication prompts. Single sign-on (SSO) reduces authentication friction. Risk-based authentication increases security requirements only when behavior deviates from normal patterns. Transparent multi-factor authentication using managed devices and behavioral biometrics verifies users without disrupting workflows.

Monitoring and Analytics

Zero Trust generates enormous amounts of access logs and authentication events. Security information and event management (SIEM) systems and user and entity behavior analytics (UEBA) platforms analyze this data to detect anomalies, identify compromised credentials, and trace attack paths.

Zero Trust Maturity Model

Organizations progress through Zero Trust maturity stages:

Traditional – Perimeter-based security with implicit trust for internal networks.

Advanced – Some Zero Trust elements like MFA and basic segmentation, but still relying primarily on perimeter security.

Optimal – Comprehensive Zero Trust implementation with identity-centric security, pervasive MFA, micro-segmentation, and continuous monitoring.

Optimal-plus – Advanced capabilities including automated response, machine learning-based threat detection, and full integration across all systems and applications.

7.5 Micro-segmentation and Least Privilege

Understanding Micro-segmentation

Micro-segmentation represents a fundamental shift from traditional network segmentation approaches. Where conventional segmentation divides networks into relatively large zones (VLANs or subnets), micro-segmentation creates granular security boundaries around individual workloads, applications, or even processes.

Traditional segmentation operates at the network layer, using IP addresses and VLANs to group resources. Micro-segmentation typically operates at the application layer, defining policies based on application identity, user identity, and contextual factors rather than network attributes. This approach remains effective as workloads migrate between on-premises and cloud environments, since policies are not tied to specific network locations.

Benefits of Micro-segmentation

Micro-segmentation dramatically reduces attack surface by limiting communications to only those explicitly permitted. Instead of allowing any system within a network segment to communicate with any other system in that segment, micro-segmentation enforces explicit, whitelist-based policies.

This approach is particularly effective against lateral movement. When attackers compromise a system, micro-segmentation prevents them from pivoting to other resources. The ransomware that encrypts one server cannot spread to others when communications between workloads are restricted. Data breaches remain contained to the initially compromised systems rather than expanding throughout the environment.

Micro-segmentation also improves compliance by demonstrating clear controls around sensitive data. Auditors can verify that cardholder data environments, protected health information, or other regulated data can only be accessed by explicitly authorized systems and users.

Implementing Micro-segmentation

Workload-Centric Policies

Micro-segmentation policies focus on workload requirements rather than network topology. Policies define which systems can communicate with a database, which services an application can access, and which users can reach management interfaces. These policies follow workloads as they move between environments.

Visibility and Mapping

Successful micro-segmentation begins with understanding existing traffic patterns. Network flow analysis tools map communications between systems, revealing dependencies and access patterns. This visibility identifies which systems actually need to communicate, distinguishing necessary communications from those that result from overly permissive firewall rules.

Application dependency mapping creates visual representations of how applications interact. These maps guide policy creation, ensuring that segmentation doesn't break application functionality. Organizations typically start by monitoring traffic in observation mode, refining policies based on actual behavior before enforcing restrictions.

Policy Enforcement Points

Micro-segmentation can be enforced at multiple layers. Host-based firewalls on individual servers provide workload-level control. Hypervisor-based enforcement in virtualized environments operates at the virtual network layer. Network-based enforcement uses distributed firewalls within software-defined networking infrastructure. Many organizations use multiple enforcement points for defense in depth.

Automation and Orchestration

Manual policy management becomes impractical as micro-segmentation scales to thousands of workloads. Modern micro-segmentation platforms provide automation capabilities that dynamically adjust policies based on workload attributes and behavior. When new workloads deploy, policies automatically apply based on security groups, tags, or labels. If workloads move to different hosts or clouds, policies follow them.

Zero Trust Network Architecture

Micro-segmentation serves as a key enabler of Zero Trust networking. By eliminating implicit trust between workloads, micro-segmentation enforces the Zero Trust principle of never trusting based on network location. Even systems in the same data center or cloud VPC must authenticate and be explicitly authorized before communicating.

The Principle of Least Privilege

Least privilege is a foundational security principle: every user, application, and system should have only the minimum permissions necessary to perform its intended functions. While simple in concept, least privilege proves challenging to implement consistently across complex environments.

Privilege Creep

Over time, user permissions tend to accumulate. When employees change roles, they often retain permissions from previous positions while gaining new ones. Rarely do organizations systematically review and revoke unnecessary access. This "privilege creep" results in users possessing far more access than their current role requires, expanding the potential impact of compromised credentials.

Over-Provisioning

Administrators often grant excessive permissions to simplify access management or preempt future access requests. Users receive group membership that provides broader access than needed. Service accounts run with system-level privileges when more restrictive permissions would suffice. These shortcuts create security risks that persist indefinitely.

Implementing Least Privilege Access

Role-Based Access Control (RBAC)

RBAC assigns permissions to roles rather than individual users. Users receive role assignments based on their job functions. When employees change positions, administrators modify role assignments rather than individual permissions. While RBAC improves consistency, it can result in role explosion as organizations create increasingly specific roles to avoid over-permissioning.

Attribute-Based Access Control (ABAC)

ABAC makes access decisions based on attributes of users, resources, and environmental context. Instead of asking "Does this user have the Accounting role?" ABAC asks "Does this user's department attribute equal 'accounting' and is their access location within the approved range?" ABAC provides more granular control than RBAC while avoiding role proliferation.

Just-in-Time (JIT) Access

JIT access grants elevated privileges only when needed and only for the duration required. Rather than permanently assigning administrative rights, JIT systems provision temporary access when administrators need to perform specific tasks. After a defined period or when administrators complete their work, elevated privileges automatically revoke. This approach dramatically reduces the window of exposure for privileged credentials.

Privileged Access Management (PAM)

PAM solutions secure, control, and monitor privileged accounts. Password vaulting stores privileged credentials centrally, rotating them regularly without requiring administrators to know the passwords. Session recording captures all privileged sessions for audit and forensic purposes. Privileged session management allows administrators to access systems without knowing passwords, automatically injecting credentials at connection time.

Service Account Management

Service accounts represent a frequently overlooked aspect of least privilege. Applications and automated processes often run with excessive permissions because administrators lack visibility into minimum required access. Service account management solutions analyze service account behavior to identify unnecessary permissions. Many modern architectures eliminate static service accounts entirely in favor of short-lived tokens and managed identities.

7.6 Regulatory and Compliance Requirements: Impact on Network Design

The Intersection of Compliance and Security Architecture

Regulatory compliance has become a primary driver of network architecture decisions across virtually all industries. While security practitioners often debate whether compliance-driven security produces optimal outcomes, the reality is that regulatory frameworks establish minimum security baselines that organizations must achieve. Understanding how major regulatory regimes impact network design enables architects to build systems that satisfy compliance requirements while implementing security best practices.

Compliance requirements influence network design through several mechanisms. They mandate specific security controls, define data handling procedures, establish audit and logging requirements, and impose geographic restrictions on data storage and processing. Organizations operating in multiple jurisdictions must navigate overlapping and sometimes conflicting regulatory requirements, creating complex design constraints.

The relationship between compliance and security is nuanced. Compliance represents a snapshot of minimum requirements at a specific point in time, while the threat landscape evolves continuously. Organizations that treat compliance as a security ceiling rather than a floor often find themselves vulnerable to emerging threats. Conversely, compliance frameworks provide structured approaches to risk management that prevent organizations from overlooking fundamental security practices.

General Data Protection Regulation (GDPR)

The European Union's General Data Protection Regulation represents one of the most comprehensive and far-reaching privacy regulations globally. While primarily focused on data protection and privacy rather than cybersecurity per se, GDPR's requirements have profound implications for network architecture and security controls.

Scope and Applicability: GDPR applies to any organization that processes personal data of EU residents, regardless of where the organization is located. This extraterritorial reach means that a company headquartered in the United States, operating cloud infrastructure in Asia, must comply with GDPR if it processes data belonging to individuals in the EU. The regulation defines personal data broadly to include any information relating to an identified or identifiable natural person, encompassing everything from names and email addresses to IP addresses and cookie identifiers.

Data Sovereignty and Geographic Restrictions: GDPR imposes restrictions on transferring personal data outside the European Economic Area (EEA) unless adequate protections exist. This requirement fundamentally impacts network design for global organizations. Architects must implement data residency controls that ensure EU resident data remains within approved geographic boundaries or is transferred only through legally sanctioned mechanisms like Standard Contractual Clauses (SCCs) or Binding Corporate Rules (BCRs).

Network designs that support GDPR compliance typically implement geographic routing and data segregation. Content delivery networks must be configured to route requests from EU users to EU-based edge locations. Cloud storage services must utilize region-specific buckets or containers with replication limited to approved jurisdictions. Data pipelines must incorporate geographic tagging to ensure analytics workloads processing EU personal data execute within compliant regions.

Data Protection by Design and by Default: Article 25 of GDPR requires that data protection measures be integrated into processing activities from the design phase and that default settings provide the highest level of privacy protection. This principle translates to network architectures that implement encryption by default, minimize data collection and retention, and enforce purpose limitation through technical controls.

Network segmentation plays a crucial role in implementing data protection by design. Personal data should reside in segregated network zones with enhanced access controls and monitoring. Systems that process personal data should have minimal network connectivity to non-essential services. Encryption should be applied both in transit and at rest, with key management systems designed to support data subject rights like the right to erasure.

Accountability and Demonstrable Compliance: GDPR emphasizes accountability, requiring organizations to demonstrate compliance rather than merely assert it. This requirement drives implementation of comprehensive logging, monitoring, and audit capabilities within network architectures. Organizations must maintain records of processing activities, conduct data protection impact assessments (DPIAs) for high-risk processing, and be able to demonstrate the effectiveness of security measures.

Network designs must incorporate centralized logging infrastructure that captures security-relevant events across all systems processing personal data. Log retention policies must balance GDPR's storage minimization principle against the need to maintain evidence of security controls. Security information and event management (SIEM) systems aggregate and analyze logs to detect potential data breaches, which must be reported to supervisory authorities within 72 hours of discovery.

Breach Notification Requirements: GDPR's stringent breach notification timelines necessitate network architectures with real-time threat detection and rapid incident response capabilities. Organizations must be able to quickly identify the scope of a breach, assess risk to data subjects, and contain the incident. This requirement drives investment in security orchestration, automation, and response (SOAR) platforms that accelerate incident triage and remediation.

Technical Implementation Examples: Consider an e-commerce platform serving EU customers. GDPR compliance might be reflected in network design through the following controls:

- Geographic traffic routing directing EU customer requests to data centers within the EEA
- Network segmentation isolating customer data storage systems with dedicated security zones
- Encryption of all customer data in transit using TLS 1.3 and at rest using AES-256
- Database query monitoring to detect and prevent unauthorized access to personal data
- Automated data retention and deletion systems that purge data according to defined retention schedules
- DDoS protection and availability controls to satisfy GDPR's integrity and availability requirements
- Comprehensive audit logging with tamper-evident storage to support accountability

Health Insurance Portability and Accountability Act (HIPAA)

The Health Insurance Portability and Accountability Act governs the handling of protected health information (PHI) in the United States. HIPAA's Security Rule establishes standards for protecting electronic PHI (ePHI), with specific technical safeguards that directly influence network architecture.

Applicability and Covered Entities: HIPAA applies to covered entities including healthcare providers, health plans, and healthcare clearinghouses, as well as business associates that handle PHI on behalf of covered entities. The business associate provisions extend HIPAA compliance obligations throughout supply chains, meaning cloud service providers, data analytics firms, and technology vendors must implement appropriate safeguards.

Technical Safeguards Requirements: The HIPAA Security Rule organizes technical safeguards into several categories that map directly to network security controls:

Access Control: HIPAA requires unique user identification, emergency access procedures, automatic logoff, and encryption and decryption mechanisms. Network designs must implement granular authentication and authorization systems that uniquely identify every individual accessing ePHI. Role-based access control systems limit access to the minimum necessary for job functions. Network access control solutions prevent unauthorized devices from connecting to networks that handle ePHI.

Multi-factor authentication has become standard for HIPAA compliance, particularly for remote access scenarios. Network architectures typically implement centralized identity providers with support for step-up authentication, where sensitive operations require additional verification. Certificate-based authentication for device trust complements user authentication to implement defense-in-depth.

Audit Controls: HIPAA mandates mechanisms that record and examine activity in systems containing ePHI. Network architectures must incorporate comprehensive logging that captures who accessed what information, when, and from where. Log aggregation systems collect data from diverse sources including network devices, servers, applications, and databases. Log integrity mechanisms prevent tampering, and log analysis systems detect suspicious access patterns.

Healthcare organizations typically implement database activity monitoring (DAM) solutions that capture all queries against systems containing ePHI. Network traffic analysis systems provide visibility into data flows involving ePHI. User and entity behavior analytics (UEBA) platforms establish baselines of normal activity and alert on deviations that might indicate insider threats or compromised accounts.

Integrity Controls: HIPAA requires mechanisms to ensure ePHI is not improperly altered or destroyed. Network architectures implement integrity controls through encryption, digital signatures, and version control systems. Checksums verify that data remains unaltered during transmission and storage. Blockchain and distributed ledger technologies are emerging as potential mechanisms for ensuring data integrity in healthcare scenarios.

Transmission Security: HIPAA explicitly requires protection of ePHI being transmitted over electronic networks. Network designs must implement encryption for all ePHI transmissions, whether over public networks or internal networks. TLS encryption for web-based applications, VPNs for site-to-site connectivity, and encrypted email solutions all support transmission security requirements.

Healthcare organizations often implement network isolation strategies where ePHI never traverses public networks directly. Private connections to cloud providers, such as AWS DirectConnect or Azure ExpressRoute, provide dedicated network paths that don't traverse the public internet. For scenarios requiring internet connectivity, organizations implement always-on VPN solutions or zero trust network access systems.

Minimum Necessary Principle: While not strictly a network architecture requirement, HIPAA's minimum necessary rule influences system design. Networks should be architected to facilitate data minimization, ensuring users and applications access only the PHI necessary for their functions. This principle aligns closely with least privilege access and micro-segmentation strategies.

Network-level data loss prevention (DLP) systems can enforce minimum necessary requirements by detecting and blocking inappropriate PHI transfers. Application proxies inspect traffic to ensure only authorized data subsets are transmitted. Masking and de-identification systems integrate with network architectures to provide anonymized data for analytics and testing purposes.

Technical Implementation Examples: A hospital network architecture reflecting HIPAA compliance might include:

- Network segmentation isolating ePHI systems into dedicated security zones with enhanced monitoring
- Role-based access control integrated with healthcare information systems to enforce minimum necessary access
- Encrypted storage for all ePHI with key management systems designed for high availability
- Comprehensive audit logging capturing all ePHI access with secure, tamper-evident log storage
- Encryption of all network communications containing ePHI using TLS 1.2 or higher
- Network access control preventing unauthorized devices from accessing clinical networks
- Data loss prevention systems detecting and preventing unauthorized ePHI transmission
- Intrusion detection and prevention systems specifically tuned for healthcare environments
- Backup and disaster recovery systems with encryption and geographic distribution

Payment Card Industry Data Security Standard (PCI DSS)

The Payment Card Industry Data Security Standard is a contractual security standard imposed by payment card brands on merchants and service providers that process, store, or transmit cardholder data. While not government regulation, PCI DSS compliance is effectively mandatory for organizations that accept payment cards, making it a critical driver of network architecture decisions in retail, e-commerce, and financial services.

Scope and Cardholder Data Environment: PCI DSS applies to the cardholder data environment (CDE), which includes systems, networks, and people that store, process, or transmit cardholder data or sensitive authentication data. A fundamental principle of PCI compliance is scope reduction—limiting the CDE to the minimum necessary systems dramatically reduces compliance burden and risk.

Network architecture is the primary mechanism for defining and limiting CDE scope. Organizations implement network segmentation to isolate systems that handle cardholder data from general corporate networks. This segmentation must be validated through network configuration review and penetration testing to ensure the CDE is genuinely isolated.

Network Segmentation and Isolation: PCI DSS Requirement 1 mandates installation and maintenance of firewall configurations to protect cardholder data. This translates to network architectures with clearly defined security zones and enforced traffic flows. The CDE should be segmented from untrusted networks (the internet) and from trusted but out-of-scope networks (corporate workstations, development environments).

Effective PCI network segmentation typically implements multiple security zones:

- External DMZ: Hosts internet-facing payment interfaces with minimal trust and heavy monitoring
- Processing Zone: Contains payment processing applications and gateways
- Data Storage Zone: Houses systems that store cardholder data, with the most restrictive access controls
- Corporate Network: General business systems explicitly isolated from the CDE
- Development/Test Network: Non-production environments that should never contain real cardholder data

Firewalls enforce traffic rules between these zones, permitting only necessary communications and denying all other traffic by default. Intrusion detection and prevention systems monitor traffic crossing zone boundaries. Jump servers or privileged access workstations provide controlled access into the CDE for authorized administrators.

Access Control and Authentication: PCI DSS requires strong access control measures including unique IDs for all users, restriction of physical and logical access to cardholder data by business need-to-know, and multi-factor authentication for all access into the CDE from untrusted networks.

Network architectures implement these requirements through centralized authentication systems with multi-factor authentication for CDE access. Network access control systems verify device compliance before permitting CDE connectivity. Privileged access management solutions control administrative access and session recording capabilities provide audit trails of administrative activities.

Zero trust principles align well with PCI access control requirements. Rather than trusting internal networks, ZTNA solutions authenticate and authorize every access request to CDE resources. This approach supports PCI compliance while enabling more flexible network architectures, particularly for cloud and hybrid environments.

Encryption and Key Management: PCI DSS mandates encryption of cardholder data transmissions over public networks and strong cryptography for stored cardholder data. Network designs must ensure all payment data transmits over encrypted channels, typically using TLS for application-layer encryption or VPNs for network-layer encryption.

Key management systems must support encryption operations while maintaining strict access controls over cryptographic keys. Hardware security modules (HSMs) provide tamper-resistant key storage and cryptographic operations. Key management architectures must support key rotation, secure backup and recovery, and audit logging of all key access.

Cloud environments present particular challenges for PCI compliance due to shared responsibility models. Organizations must carefully evaluate cloud providers' PCI attestations, implement additional controls where necessary, and maintain clear documentation of control responsibilities. Network architectures in cloud environments often leverage cloud-native security services while implementing additional monitoring and encryption to satisfy PCI requirements.

Vulnerability Management and Testing: PCI DSS requires regular vulnerability scanning by Approved Scanning Vendors (ASVs) for external networks and internal vulnerability assessments. Network architectures must facilitate these scanning activities while preventing scan traffic from impacting production systems.

Penetration testing requirements demand that network segmentation be validated annually and after significant changes. Network designs should anticipate these testing requirements, providing mechanisms for testers to safely conduct assessments without risking production data or availability.

Logging and Monitoring: PCI Requirement 10 mandates comprehensive logging of all access to cardholder data and network resources. Log aggregation systems must collect data from all CDE systems with time synchronization across the environment. Log review processes, whether manual or automated, must identify and respond to anomalies.

Security information and event management (SIEM) systems serve as central logging platforms for PCI environments, correlating events across diverse systems to detect potential compromise. File integrity monitoring (FIM) systems detect unauthorized changes to critical system files. Network behavior analysis systems establish baselines and alert on deviations.

Technical Implementation Examples: An e-commerce company's PCI-compliant network architecture might include:

- External firewall protecting payment application servers in a DMZ
- Web application firewall inspecting all traffic to payment pages

- Internal firewall isolating the payment processing zone from corporate networks
- Encrypted communication channels for all cardholder data transmission
- Network access control restricting CDE access to authorized devices
- Centralized authentication with multi-factor authentication for CDE access
- Intrusion detection systems monitoring all CDE network segments
- SIEM platform aggregating logs from all CDE systems
- Jump server architecture for administrative access to CDE systems
- Network segmentation validated through annual penetration testing

Comparative Analysis and Multi-Regulatory Compliance

Organizations frequently operate under multiple regulatory regimes simultaneously. A healthcare provider accepting payment cards must comply with both HIPAA and PCI DSS. A European financial services firm might need to satisfy GDPR, PCI DSS, and financial regulations. This regulatory complexity drives network architecture decisions toward frameworks that satisfy multiple requirements efficiently.

Common Security Control Themes: Despite different focus areas, major regulatory frameworks share common security control requirements:

- Network Segmentation: All major frameworks benefit from or explicitly require network segmentation to isolate sensitive data
- Encryption: Data encryption, both in transit and at rest, appears across regulatory requirements
- Access Control: Principle of least privilege, unique user identification, and authentication requirements are universal

- Logging and Monitoring: Comprehensive audit logging and security monitoring support multiple compliance obligations
- Incident Response: Capabilities to detect, respond to, and report security incidents span regulatory frameworks

By implementing robust baseline security controls that satisfy the most stringent requirements across applicable regulations, organizations can achieve efficient compliance without implementing entirely separate systems for each framework.

Harmonization Strategies: Forward-thinking organizations approach compliance through harmonization strategies that identify control overlaps and implement unified systems satisfying multiple requirements. A single, well-designed identity and access management system can support access control requirements across GDPR, HIPAA, and PCI DSS. Comprehensive logging infrastructure serves audit requirements across multiple frameworks.

Network architecture becomes the foundation for regulatory harmonization. Micro-segmentation strategies support HIPAA's minimum necessary requirement, PCI's CDE isolation mandate, and GDPR's data protection by design principle. Zero trust network access satisfies authentication and authorization requirements across frameworks while providing superior security compared to perimeter-based models.

Cloud Compliance Challenges: Cloud adoption introduces additional compliance complexity. Organizations must understand cloud provider responsibility matrices and verify that cloud services meet regulatory requirements. Network architectures in cloud environments must compensate for reduced visibility and control compared to on-premises infrastructure.

Cloud-native security services provide compliance-relevant capabilities like encryption key management, network traffic logging, and security policy enforcement. However, organizations remain ultimately responsible for compliance even when leveraging cloud services. Network designs must incorporate additional monitoring, logging, and control mechanisms to satisfy regulatory requirements.

Multi-cloud strategies compound compliance challenges, as organizations must ensure consistent security controls across diverse cloud platforms. Network architectures that abstract underlying cloud infrastructure through consistent security policy enforcement layers help maintain compliance in complex environments.

Emerging Regulatory Trends

The regulatory landscape continues to evolve in response to emerging technologies and threat vectors. Several trends are shaping future network architecture requirements:

Data Localization Requirements: Beyond GDPR, numerous jurisdictions are implementing data sovereignty requirements mandating that certain data remain within geographic boundaries. China's Cybersecurity Law, Russia's data localization requirements, and various sector-specific regulations are driving network designs with geographic routing capabilities and regional data storage.

Artificial Intelligence Governance: Emerging AI regulations, including the EU AI Act, will impact network architectures that support AI systems. Requirements for transparency, explainability, and oversight may necessitate enhanced logging and monitoring of AI system behavior. Network isolation strategies may separate AI training environments from production systems to prevent data leakage and ensure model integrity.

Supply Chain Security Requirements: Regulations increasingly address supply chain security, requiring organizations to assess and monitor third-party vendors. Network architectures must support vendor risk management through capabilities like vendor-specific network segments, enhanced monitoring of vendor access, and controls preventing vendors from moving laterally beyond authorized systems.

Zero Trust Mandates: Government agencies, particularly in the United States, are mandating zero trust architectures. While not traditional regulations, these mandates influence commercial network design as vendors seek to support government customers. The practical effect is accelerated adoption of zero trust principles across industries.

Breach Notification Harmonization: As breach notification requirements proliferate globally, organizations are implementing network architectures with standardized incident detection and response capabilities. Rather than customizing systems for each jurisdiction's notification requirements, organizations build comprehensive breach detection capabilities that exceed any single regulatory requirement.

Compliance as a Catalyst for Security Excellence

While compliance should not be mistaken for security, regulatory requirements have undeniably improved baseline security practices across industries. Organizations that might otherwise underinvest in security are compelled by regulation to implement fundamental controls. Compliance audits provide structured frameworks for assessing security posture and identifying gaps.

The most successful organizations view compliance as a floor rather than a ceiling, implementing security controls that exceed regulatory minimums. They leverage compliance frameworks as structured approaches to risk management while supplementing them with threat-informed security practices. Network architectures designed with both compliance and security in mind provide defensible infrastructures that satisfy auditors while protecting against real-world threats.

Regulatory requirements will continue shaping network architecture decisions, but the ultimate goal remains protecting organizational assets and customer data from compromise. By understanding how regulations translate to technical requirements, security architects can design networks that achieve compliance efficiently while implementing security best practices that defend against evolving threats.

Chapter 8

Securing the Internet of Things (IoT) Ecosystem

8.1 Introduction

The Internet of Things represents one of the most transformative technological shifts of the twenty-first century, fundamentally altering how physical and digital worlds interact. From smart home devices and wearable health monitors to industrial control systems and smart city infrastructure, IoT devices have proliferated across every sector of modern society. Analysts estimate that by 2025, there will be over 15-20 billion connected IoT devices worldwide, generating unprecedented volumes of data and creating vast attack surfaces that traditional security paradigms struggle to address.

The security implications of IoT proliferation are profound and multifaceted. Unlike traditional computing devices designed with security as a foundational consideration, many IoT devices prioritize functionality, cost efficiency, and power conservation over security. This design philosophy has resulted in ecosystems of devices with minimal processing power, constrained memory, limited update mechanisms, and often, virtually no security controls. The consequences of IoT insecurity extend beyond data breaches to encompass physical safety risks, as compromised devices can affect critical infrastructure, medical equipment, and transportation systems.

IoT security challenges are exacerbated by the heterogeneity of the ecosystem. Devices span enormous diversity in computational capability, from resource-constrained sensors running on coin-cell batteries to powerful industrial gateways with multi-core processors. Communication protocols range from Bluetooth Low Energy and Zigbee to cellular networks and satellite connectivity. Operating systems include everything from bare-metal firmware to embedded Linux distributions. This fragmentation makes implementing uniform security policies and controls extraordinarily difficult.

Traditional enterprise security tools and practices often prove inadequate for IoT environments. Network security appliances designed to inspect and filter traditional IT traffic may lack visibility into specialized IoT protocols. Endpoint security solutions requiring agent installation cannot function on devices with limited processing power or proprietary operating systems. Vulnerability management processes built around regular patching cycles break down when confronting devices with ten-year operational lifespans and manufacturers that abandon support after initial sale.

This chapter examines the unique security challenges posed by IoT ecosystems and explores architectural approaches to securing them. We begin with an analysis of the fundamental constraints that differentiate IoT security from traditional cybersecurity, then progress through device onboarding and authentication mechanisms, the role of SD-WAN in connecting distributed IoT deployments, network segmentation strategies for isolating IoT and operational technology networks, and behavioral monitoring techniques for detecting compromised devices. Throughout, we emphasize practical, implementable security controls that acknowledge IoT constraints while providing meaningful risk reduction.

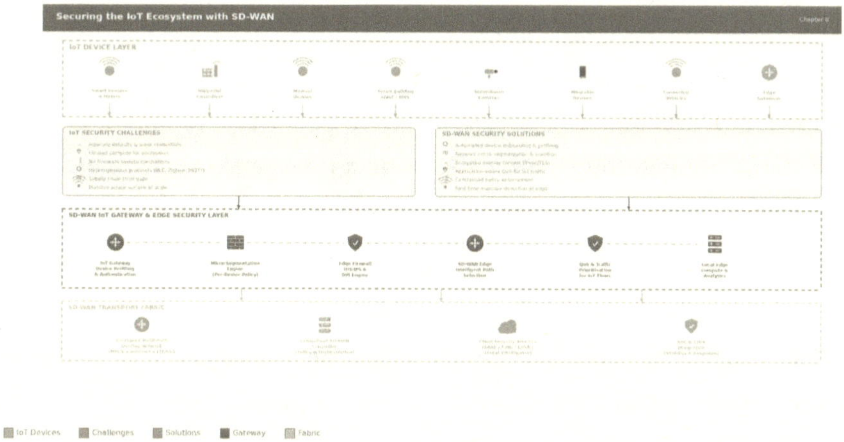

Figure 8.1: Securing IoT Ecosystems with SD-WAN — End-to-End Architecture

8.2 Unique Security Challenges of IoT Devices

Resource Constraints and Security Trade-offs

The defining characteristic of many IoT devices is severe resource constraint. Unlike traditional computing platforms with gigabytes of RAM and multi-core processors, IoT devices often operate with kilobytes of memory and microcontrollers measured in megahertz rather than gigahertz. These constraints fundamentally limit what security controls can be implemented.

Computational Limitations: Cryptographic operations that execute instantaneously on modern computers may be prohibitively expensive on resource-constrained devices. Public key cryptography, which forms the foundation of secure communications and authentication in traditional systems, requires significant computational resources. A single RSA signature verification might consume seconds on a low-power microcontroller, creating unacceptable latency for time-sensitive applications.

These computational constraints force difficult trade-offs between security and functionality. Lightweight cryptographic algorithms designed for constrained environments offer reduced security margins compared to their full-strength counterparts. Elliptic curve cryptography provides better security-per-computational-cost than RSA, making it preferable for IoT applications, but even ECC operations strain the capabilities of the most resource-limited devices.

Consider a wireless sensor node deployed in an agricultural monitoring application. The device might operate on battery power for years, sampling soil conditions and transmitting data periodically. Every cryptographic operation consumes precious battery capacity. Designers must balance security requirements against operational longevity, potentially accepting weaker encryption or less frequent authentication to extend battery life.

Memory Limitations: IoT devices frequently operate with 256KB or less of flash memory for program storage and 64KB or less of RAM for runtime operations. These constraints severely limit the complexity of security protocols and algorithms that can be implemented. Security libraries that occupy tens of megabytes in traditional environments simply cannot fit on IoT devices.

Memory constraints also affect the ability to implement security-critical features like secure boot sequences, which verify firmware authenticity before execution. Cryptographic key storage competes with application functionality for scarce memory resources. Buffer overflow protections and runtime security checks that modern operating systems provide are often absent due to memory and performance overhead.

The limited memory also constrains logging and monitoring capabilities. Devices may lack capacity to maintain meaningful security logs or retain forensic evidence of compromise. This absence of audit trails impedes incident detection and response, as security teams have minimal visibility into device behavior and historical activity.

Power Consumption Constraints: Many IoT devices operate on battery power or harvest energy from environmental sources. Power consumption directly impacts device operational lifetime and, in some cases, determines whether a deployment is economically viable. Security mechanisms that increase power consumption face significant adoption barriers.

Radio communication typically represents the dominant power consumer in wireless IoT devices. Security protocols that increase communication overhead – through larger packet sizes due to encryption headers or additional messages for authentication—directly reduce battery life. Cryptographic operations also consume power, though typically less than radio transmission.

These power constraints create perverse incentives where manufacturers may disable security features to achieve longer battery life or choose protocols with minimal security overhead. Devices shipped with default credentials that are never changed, lack of encryption for sensitive data transmission, and absence of authentication mechanisms are all frequently justified by power consumption concerns.

Fragmented Update Cycles and Patch Management Challenges

The IoT ecosystem suffers from catastrophic fragmentation in update mechanisms and patch management practices. Unlike traditional IT environments where operating systems and applications receive regular security updates through standardized mechanisms, IoT devices often lack any update capability whatsoever. When update mechanisms exist, they frequently suffer from serious security vulnerabilities or operational challenges that prevent effective patching.

Absence of Update Mechanisms: A substantial portion of deployed IoT devices have no capability for firmware updates after initial deployment. This design choice reflects cost optimization, power constraints, or simply inadequate security consideration during product development.

Devices expected to operate for decades without maintenance cannot receive security patches addressing newly discovered vulnerabilities.

The implications are profound. A vulnerability discovered in a widely deployed IoT device with no update mechanism represents a permanent security defect that will persist throughout the device's operational lifetime. Organizations deploying such devices must implement compensating controls at the network level, as the devices themselves cannot be secured.

Insecure Update Mechanisms: Even when update capabilities exist, many implementations suffer from critical security flaws. Unsigned firmware updates allow attackers to install malicious software on devices. Update mechanisms lacking encrypted communication expose firmware to interception and analysis, potentially revealing intellectual property or enabling development of exploits. Authentication failures in update processes allow unauthorized parties to modify device software.

The Mirai botnet, which compromised hundreds of thousands of IoT devices to launch massive distributed denial-of-service attacks, exploited devices with weak default credentials and absent or ineffective security update mechanisms. Many compromised devices could have been secured through firmware updates, but manufacturers lacked mechanisms to push updates or users lacked awareness of how to apply them.

Update Fragmentation Across Vendors: The IoT ecosystem lacks standardized update mechanisms comparable to operating system update frameworks in traditional IT. Each manufacturer implements proprietary update processes, if any exist at all. This fragmentation creates operational challenges for organizations managing diverse device fleets, as security teams must maintain awareness of update procedures across potentially hundreds of device types.

Cloud-connected devices may receive automatic updates through vendor-managed platforms, but this approach introduces dependency on vendor operational continuity. If a manufacturer ceases operations or discontinues cloud service support, devices may become permanently unmaintainable. The rapid consolidation and frequent start-up failures in the IoT industry have created graveyards of orphaned devices receiving no security support.

Long Device Lifecycles: IoT devices in industrial and infrastructure applications often operate for decades. Manufacturing equipment, building automation systems, and utility infrastructure may have twenty-year or longer operational lifespans. Contrast this with traditional IT equipment typically refreshed every three to five years.

These extended lifecycles create fundamental mismatches with security update practices. Manufacturers frequently discontinue security support for products well before their operational end-of-life. A device deployed in 2020 and expected to operate until 2040 may receive security updates only through 2025, leaving fifteen years of unsupported operation where newly discovered vulnerabilities cannot be addressed.

The long lifecycle also means devices may outlive the cryptographic algorithms and protocols considered secure at deployment time. A device deployed today using current cryptographic standards may find those standards deprecated or broken before the device reaches end-of-life, but lack the capability to upgrade to newer algorithms.

8.3 Insecure Defaults and Credential Management Failures

IoT security is plagued by pervasive use of insecure default configurations and credential management practices that would be considered catastrophic in traditional IT environments yet remain disturbingly common in IoT deployments.

Default Credentials: Countless IoT devices ship with default usernames and passwords that are widely known, easily guessable, or even hardcoded into firmware. Manufacturers use default credentials like "admin/admin" or "root/password" to simplify initial device setup, expecting users to change them. In practice, vast numbers of devices remain configured with default credentials throughout their operational lifetime.

The security implications are severe. Attackers maintain databases of default credentials for thousands of device models. Automated scanning tools continuously probe internet-connected devices, attempting authentication with known default credentials. Successful authentication grants complete control over devices, enabling their incorporation into botnets, data exfiltration, or use as pivot points for deeper network penetration.

Some devices implement default credentials that cannot be changed by users—hardcoded credentials embedded in firmware or derived from device serial numbers through predictable algorithms. These design choices make mass compromise trivial, as a single set of credentials or credential generation algorithm provides access to every device of a particular model.

Lack of Credential Uniqueness: Even when devices allow credential changes, manufacturers often use identical default credentials across all devices of a model. This practice means that discovering default credentials for one device immediately compromises all similar devices. Best practice would assign unique default credentials to each device, forcing attackers to compromise devices individually rather than large scale.

Certificate-based authentication, which could provide unique device identities, is often absent from IoT devices due to cost, complexity, or computational constraints. Pre-shared key approaches might use identical keys across all devices, eliminating the security benefit of cryptographic authentication.

Inadequate Authentication Mechanisms: Many IoT devices implement authentication mechanisms with serious security deficiencies.

Protocols that transmit credentials in plaintext over unencrypted connections expose them to interception. Inadequate account lockout policies allow brute-force attacks. Absence of multi-factor authentication makes credential compromise the only barrier to device access.

Web management interfaces on IoT devices frequently exhibit vulnerabilities that would be considered elementary in web application security: SQL injection, cross-site scripting, cross-site request forgery, and authentication bypass vulnerabilities. These defects reflect inadequate security expertise among device manufacturers, many of whom excel in their core domain (e.g., HVAC systems, industrial sensors) but lack cybersecurity knowledge.

8.4 Protocol Vulnerabilities and Communication Security

IoT devices communicate using diverse protocols spanning multiple layers of the network stack. Many of these protocols were designed prioritizing factors like power efficiency, range, or interoperability over security. The result is an ecosystem rife with insecure communication channels.

Unencrypted Communication: Substantial numbers of IoT devices transmit sensitive data without encryption. Sensor readings, control commands, configuration information, and even credentials may traverse networks in plaintext. This lack of encryption stems from computational constraints, protocol limitations, or simply absent security consideration during design.

Unencrypted communication enables passive eavesdropping where attackers gain access to sensitive information without actively compromising devices. Traffic analysis can reveal activity patterns even without understanding specific message content. Man-in-the-middle attacks allow active interception and modification of communications, potentially altering sensor readings or injecting malicious commands.

Weak Cryptographic Implementations: When IoT devices do implement encryption, the implementations often suffer from serious weaknesses. Use of deprecated algorithms like DES or RC4 provides minimal security against modern cryptanalytic techniques. Short key lengths that were adequate when protocols were designed have become vulnerable to brute-force attacks. Predictable initialization vectors and nonces undermine encryption schemes that depend on randomness.

Protocol implementations may exhibit subtle vulnerabilities arising from incorrect use of cryptographic primitives. Padding oracle attacks, timing side-channels, and state confusion vulnerabilities have affected numerous IoT protocols. The specialized knowledge required to implement cryptography correctly is often absent from IoT development teams.

Protocol-Specific Vulnerabilities: IoT-specific communication protocols like Zigbee, Z-Wave, LoRaWAN, and Thread each have unique security characteristics and vulnerabilities. Zigbee's network key management has exhibited vulnerabilities allowing key extraction. Z-Wave's initial iterations lacked encryption entirely. LoRaWAN's join procedures have been subject to various attacks. Understanding the security implications of each protocol requires specialized knowledge that many organizations deploying IoT devices lack.

Bluetooth Low Energy, widely used in consumer IoT devices, has evolved through multiple versions with varying security capabilities. Pairing mechanisms suffer from vulnerabilities to eavesdropping and man-in-the-middle attacks. Legacy devices using older Bluetooth versions may have fundamental security limitations that cannot be addressed without hardware replacement.

8.5 Supply Chain Security and Hardware Trust

IoT device security begins long before deployment, with supply chain integrity and hardware trustworthiness representing foundational concerns. Unlike software vulnerabilities that can potentially be patched, hardware-level compromises or supply chain attacks may be impossible to remediate.

Component-Level Vulnerabilities: IoT devices incorporate components from global supply chains with varying security standards. Microcontrollers, communication modules, and sensors may contain vulnerabilities or backdoors introduced during manufacturing. The complexity of modern semiconductor manufacturing, with design, fabrication, and assembly occurring across multiple countries and companies, creates numerous opportunities for compromise.

Counterfeit components represent another supply chain risk. Substandard or recycled components may lack security features of genuine parts or exhibit reliability issues that create security vulnerabilities. Organizations purchasing devices through unofficial channels or at suspiciously low prices risk acquiring products with counterfeit components.

Firmware and Software Integrity: IoT devices are programmed with firmware during manufacturing, creating opportunities for malicious code introduction. Contract manufacturers or component suppliers with access to firmware images could modify them to include backdoors. Software development tool compromises could inject malicious code into builds without developers' knowledge, as demonstrated by sophisticated supply chain attacks against traditional software.

The absence of secure boot mechanisms in many IoT devices means that even if firmware ships uncompromised, attackers with physical access can replace it with malicious versions. Without cryptographic verification of firmware authenticity, devices have no mechanism to detect unauthorized modifications.

Physical Security Limitations: IoT devices deployed in uncontrolled environments face physical security threats uncommon in traditional IT. Devices mounted on utility poles, deployed in agricultural fields, or installed in public spaces may be accessible to attackers who can physically tamper with them. Hardware debugging interfaces left enabled in production devices provide direct access to device memory and execution flow.

Side-channel attacks against IoT devices can extract cryptographic keys through analysis of power consumption, electromagnetic emissions, or timing variations. Resource-constrained devices often lack countermeasures against such attacks due to implementation overhead. Physical attacks on secure elements or trusted platform modules can compromise cryptographic roots of trust.

8.6 Privacy Implications of IoT Data Collection

IoT devices frequently collect intimate data about individuals' behaviors, locations, health status, and living environments. The aggregation of data from multiple IoT sources enables detailed surveillance and behavioral profiling that raises profound privacy concerns.

Sensor Data Sensitivity: Individual sensor readings may appear innocuous, but aggregated data reveals sensitive patterns. Smart meter data discloses when residents are home and what appliances they use. Fitness trackers expose health information and location history. Connected vehicles create detailed records of travel patterns. Voice assistants record conversations in private spaces.

The granularity and volume of IoT data collection exceed traditional surveillance capabilities. Sensors sample data at high frequencies, creating temporal resolution that reveals fine-grained behavioral patterns. The persistence of data storage means that information collected today may be analyzed years later using techniques that don't exist at collection time.

Data Minimization Challenges: Privacy-preserving design principles advocate collecting only data necessary for specific purposes, but IoT implementations often violate this principle. Manufacturers collect extensive telemetry about device usage for product improvement or analytics purposes. Cloud platforms aggregate data from multiple users to train machine learning models. The economic incentives around data collection encourage maximalist approaches that gather everything possible.

Limited processing power on edge devices complicates privacy-preserving approaches like differential privacy or federated learning that require computational resources for local processing. Encrypted computation techniques that would allow data analysis without exposing individual records are often too computationally expensive for IoT platforms.

Third-Party Data Sharing: IoT ecosystems frequently involve data sharing among manufacturers, cloud service providers, analytics platforms, and application developers. Privacy policies often grant broad rights for data sharing that user don't understand or expect. The complexity of data flows through IoT ecosystems makes it difficult for even sophisticated users to comprehend how their data is used.

Cross-device tracking and behavioral profiling across services create privacy risks that extend beyond individual device capabilities. A manufacturer collecting data from smart home devices, wearables, and connected vehicles for a single user can construct comprehensive behavioral profiles. Data brokers aggregate IoT data from multiple sources to enhance their commercial profiles of individuals.

8.7 IoT Device Onboarding and Authentication

Secure device onboarding and authentication represent critical foundations for IoT security. Establishing device identity, provisioning credentials, and authenticating devices attempting network or service access must occur in ways that balance security requirements against the practical constraints of IoT deployments.

Device Identity and Lifecycle Management

Before devices can be secured, they must possess unique, verifiable identities that persist throughout their operational lifetime. Device identity serves as the foundation for authentication, authorization, and audit functions within IoT ecosystems.

Unique Device Identifiers: Every IoT device requires a unique identifier that distinguishes it from all other devices. Simple approaches use hardware addresses like MAC addresses or manufacturer serial numbers, but these identifiers often lack cryptographic binding to device hardware and may be spoofable. More robust approaches implement cryptographic identities based on public-private key pairs generated during device manufacturing.

Hardware-based unique device secrets (UDS) embedded during chip manufacturing provide cryptographically strong device identities that resist cloning or modification. These secrets serve as roots of trust for deriving operational credentials and establishing secure channels. Physical unclonable functions (PUFs) leverage microscopic manufacturing variations to generate unique device-specific keys that don't require storage in non-volatile memory, reducing vulnerability to physical attacks.

Identity Lifecycle Management: Device identity must be managed throughout the device lifecycle from manufacturing through deployment, operation, and eventual decommissioning. Manufacturing processes provision initial credentials and configure security parameters. Ownership transfer mechanisms allow devices to be reassigned between organizations or users without compromising security. Decommissioning processes revoke credentials and remove devices from trusted device registries.

Device identity management systems maintain registries of authorized devices with their associated credentials, certificates, and attributes. These registries support authentication decisions and provide audit trails of device activities. Cloud-based device identity platforms like Azure IoT Hub Device Provisioning Service or AWS IoT Device Management provide scalable identity management for large IoT deployments.

Certificate-Based Authentication

X.509 certificate-based authentication represents the cryptographically strongest approach to IoT device authentication, providing mutual authentication, forward secrecy, and protection against man-in-the-middle attacks. However, certificate-based approaches require computational resources and infrastructure that may exceed capabilities of the most constrained devices.

Public Key Infrastructure for IoT: Implementing PKI for IoT devices requires certificate authorities dedicated to device certificates with lifecycle management appropriate for IoT use cases. Device certificates typically have longer validity periods than traditional PKI to reduce the operational burden of renewal, though this practice increases risk from compromised certificates.

Certificate enrollment can occur during manufacturing, where device key pairs are generated and certificate signing requests submitted to the manufacturer's CA. Alternatively, devices may generate key pairs post-deployment and submit CSRs through secure enrollment protocols. The enrollment process must protect private keys from exposure, ideally generating them within hardware security modules or secure elements that never export key material.

Lightweight Certificate Formats: Traditional X.509 certificates designed for web PKI contain extensive metadata that may be unnecessarily verbose for IoT applications. Compressed certificate formats reduce storage and transmission requirements while maintaining essential security properties. Certificate chains can be abbreviated when all parties share knowledge of intermediate certificates, reducing bandwidth consumption during TLS handshakes.

Some IoT protocols implement alternative certificate formats optimized for constrained devices. CBOR Object Signing and Encryption (COSE) provides compact encoding of credentials and cryptographic operations. Raw public keys, where devices exchange public keys directly without certificate wrappers, eliminate certificate parsing overhead at the cost of simplified revocation and attribute binding.

Certificate Revocation Challenges: Traditional certificate revocation mechanisms like Certificate Revocation Lists (CRLs) and Online Certificate Status Protocol (OCSP) present challenges for IoT devices. Constrained devices may lack resources to store and process CRLs. Intermittently connected devices cannot perform real-time OCSP checks. The requirement for reliable network connectivity for revocation checking conflicts with operational realities of many IoT deployments.

Alternative approaches to revocation in IoT environments include short-lived certificates that expire quickly enough that revocation becomes unnecessary, though this requires reliable certificate renewal mechanisms. Certificate pinning, where devices trust only specific certificates rather than broader CAs, reduces reliance on revocation infrastructure. Status verification at network gateways rather than individual devices centralizes revocation checking at more capable systems.

Token-Based Authentication

Token-based authentication provides lighter-weight alternatives to certificate-based approaches, trading some security properties for reduced computational and bandwidth requirements. JSON Web Tokens (JWT) and similar bearer token schemes are widely used in IoT platforms.

Symmetric Key Tokens: Devices and authentication servers share symmetric keys used to generate and verify authentication tokens. Devices present tokens proving they possess the shared key without transmitting the key itself. This approach requires less computation than public key cryptography, making it suitable for constrained devices.

The challenge with symmetric key approaches is key distribution and management. Secure channels must exist for provisioning shared keys into devices. Key compromise affects all devices sharing the same key, making key rotation and revocation critical. Unique per-device keys provide better security isolation but increase management complexity.

JSON Web Tokens: JWT-based authentication is popular in cloud-connected IoT deployments. Devices authenticate to receive signed JWTs that authorize subsequent API access. Tokens contain claims about device identity and permissions, encoded in JSON and digitally signed. Recipients verify token signatures without contacting the issuing authority, enabling distributed authentication checks.

JWT implementations for IoT must carefully consider token lifetime, refresh mechanisms, and the risk of token theft. Long-lived tokens reduce authentication overhead but increase risk if compromised. Short-lived tokens with refresh tokens balance security and efficiency but require devices to maintain connectivity for token renewal. Binding tokens to device-specific attributes or network contexts can limit utility of stolen tokens.

Hardware Roots of Trust

Hardware-based security modules provide cryptographically strong foundations for device authentication, key storage, and secure execution. These hardware roots of trust resist software-based attacks and provide assurance about device identity and integrity.

Trusted Platform Modules: TPM chips implement standardized hardware security functionality including secure key generation and storage, cryptographic operations, and platform integrity measurement. TPMs provide isolated execution environments where security-critical operations occur protected from potentially compromised host software.

For IoT applications, discrete TPM chips may be too expensive or consume too much power. Firmware TPMs (fTPM) and integrated TPMs provide subset functionality with lower cost and power profiles. These implementations trade some physical security for improved economics and device integration.

Secure Elements: Secure elements are tamper-resistant chips designed specifically for storing cryptographic keys and executing security-sensitive code. Originally developed for smart cards and payment applications, secure elements have found increasing application in IoT devices requiring strong hardware security.

Secure elements provide isolated environments for key generation, storage, and cryptographic operations. Private keys never leave the secure element, preventing extraction even if device firmware is compromised. Secure elements may implement countermeasures against physical attacks including invasive probing, fault injection, and side-channel analysis.

Hardware Security Modules: For high-value IoT deployments like industrial control systems or critical infrastructure, dedicated hardware security modules provide enterprise-grade cryptographic key protection. HSMs offer FIPS-validated cryptographic operations, high-performance key operations, and robust physical security.

HSMs in IoT architectures typically reside at gateways or management systems rather than individual devices due to cost constraints. Gateways equipped with HSMs can perform cryptographic operations on behalf of simpler devices, extending hardware-based security benefits across device fleets. This approach creates hierarchical trust models where constrained devices establish trust relationships with capable gateways possessing hardware roots of trust.

ARM TrustZone and TEE: Trusted Execution Environments (TEE) based on ARM TrustZone technology partition processor execution into secure and non-secure worlds. Security-sensitive code executes in the secure world, isolated from potentially compromised normal-world software. TrustZone provides hardware-enforced isolation without requiring discrete security chips.

IoT devices based on ARM processors can leverage TrustZone to protect cryptographic keys, implement secure boot, and isolate security-critical firmware. The approach provides hardware-backed security at lower cost than discrete secure elements, though with less physical tamper resistance. GlobalPlatform TEE standards enable portable security applications across TrustZone-enabled devices from multiple manufacturers.

Secure Device Provisioning

The process of provisioning devices with credentials, configuration, and authorization establishes their initial security posture. Provisioning must occur securely to prevent devices from being compromised before they even become operational.

Zero-Touch Provisioning: Automated provisioning mechanisms allow devices to self-configure when connected to networks without manual configuration. Devices contact provisioning services using bootstrap credentials embedded during manufacturing, receive operational credentials and configuration, then transition to normal operation. Zero-touch provisioning reduces operational costs for large deployments while minimizing opportunities for configuration errors.

Provisioning services authenticate devices using manufacturer certificates or hardware-based device identities before providing operational credentials. The provisioning process should establish mutual trust, with devices verifying they're communicating with legitimate provisioning servers through server certificate validation or pre-configured pinning.

Ownership Vouchers and Attestation: FIDO Device Onboard and similar protocols implement ownership voucher mechanisms where manufacturers cryptographically sign documents asserting device authenticity and initial ownership. When devices contact provisioning services, they present ownership vouchers proving they originated from legitimate manufacturers. Ownership vouchers can be transferred through distribution channels, allowing resellers to provision devices without manufacturer involvement.

Attestation during provisioning enables services to verify device integrity before granting access. Devices present measurements of their boot sequence and runtime configuration, cryptographically signed by hardware roots of trust. Provisioning services compare measurements against known-good values to detect compromised devices. Attestation provides assurance that devices run authentic, unmodified firmware before granting them access to production networks.

Credential Rotation and Renewal: Provisioning establishes initial credentials, but ongoing credential lifecycle management maintains security over device operational lifetime. Credentials should be rotated periodically to limit exposure from potential compromise. Automated renewal processes refresh credentials before expiration, preventing service disruption.

Certificate-based systems require renewal mechanisms where devices generate new key pairs and obtain updated certificates before existing certificates expire. Token-based systems implement refresh tokens allowing devices to obtain new access tokens without full re-authentication. Symmetric key rotation must coordinate key updates between devices and authentication infrastructure to prevent service disruption.

The challenge of credential rotation in IoT environments stems from connectivity constraints and device computational limitations. Intermittently connected devices may miss renewal windows. Constrained devices may lack resources to maintain multiple credential sets during rotation. Renewal mechanisms must accommodate these realities while maintaining security.

8.8 SD-WAN for Remote and Distributed IoT Gateways

The Role of IoT Gateways in Distributed Deployments

IoT gateways serve as critical intermediaries between resource-constrained edge devices and cloud or data center infrastructure. These gateways aggregate data from multiple IoT devices, perform protocol translation, implement security controls, and provide reliable connectivity to backend systems. In geographically distributed deployments—smart cities, industrial facilities, agricultural operations, retail chains—gateways deployed at remote sites face unique networking and security challenges that Software-Defined Wide Area Networking (SD-WAN) is uniquely positioned to address.

Gateway Architecture and Functions: IoT gateways typically implement multi-tier architectures where constrained devices communicate using low-power protocols (Bluetooth, Zigbee, LoRaWAN) to nearby gateways, which then aggregate and forward data over IP networks to cloud platforms. Gateways translate between diverse protocols, enabling interoperability across heterogeneous device ecosystems.

Beyond protocol translation, gateways implement edge processing capabilities that reduce bandwidth consumption and latency. Local data filtering discards redundant or low-value information before transmission. Edge analytics extract insights from raw sensor streams, transmitting only actionable intelligence. Machine learning inference at the edge enables real-time decision-making without cloud round-trips.

Security functions at gateways include terminating encrypted connections from devices, performing authentication and authorization, implementing firewall and intrusion detection capabilities, and establishing secure tunnels to cloud infrastructure. Gateways serve as security enforcement points, applying controls to devices that lack resources for sophisticated security mechanisms.

Connectivity Challenges: Gateways in remote locations face connectivity challenges uncommon in traditional enterprise environments.

Locations may have limited or unreliable internet connectivity through cellular networks, satellite links, or commodity broadband services. Multiple connectivity options may exist with varying cost, performance, and reliability characteristics. Connectivity may experience intermittent failures requiring resilient architectures that gracefully handle disconnection.

Traditional WAN architectures based on MPLS circuits provide predictable performance but at costs prohibitive for distributed IoT deployments. The economics of IoT often require leveraging lower-cost connectivity options like broadband internet or LTE, accepting reduced reliability and performance in exchange for affordable scaling to thousands of locations.

SD-WAN Fundamentals and IoT Application

Software-Defined WAN technology decouples network control from physical infrastructure, enabling centralized management of distributed networks while leveraging diverse connectivity options. SD-WAN's characteristics align well with IoT gateway connectivity requirements, providing cost-effective, resilient, manageable wide-area networking.

Control and Data Plane Separation: SD-WAN architectures separate control plane functions (routing decisions, policy definition, network orchestration) from data plane functions (packet forwarding, encryption, quality-of-service enforcement). Centralized controllers maintain network topology awareness and disseminate policies to distributed edge devices. Edge devices—in IoT contexts, typically integrated into or colocated with IoT gateways—implement data plane forwarding based on controller-provided policies.

This separation enables dynamic network configuration responsive to changing conditions. When link failures occur, controllers rapidly recompute optimal paths and push updated policies to affected devices. When new gateways are deployed, they automatically discover controllers and receive appropriate configurations. Application-aware routing policies adapt forwarding behavior based on traffic characteristics and business requirements.

Transport Independence: SD-WAN overlays run over arbitrary IP connectivity, abstracting applications and devices from underlying transport details. A single logical network spans MPLS circuits, broadband internet connections, LTE links, and satellite communications. Applications remain unaware of underlying transport diversity; the SD-WAN layer handles path selection, failover, and performance optimization.

For IoT gateways, transport independence enables flexible deployment models. Locations with fiber connectivity use high-bandwidth, low-latency links for primary communication. Locations in remote areas rely on LTE or satellite links. Budget-constrained deployments use residential broadband services. The SD-WAN layer ensures consistent connectivity regardless of underlying transport.

Multi-Path Forwarding and Active-Active Links: Unlike traditional WAN routers that designate primary and backup links, SD-WAN devices can actively utilize multiple links simultaneously. Traffic is distributed across available paths based on application requirements, link characteristics, and business policies. Voice and video traffic preferring low latency might route over one link while bulk data transfers utilize another.

For IoT applications generating diverse traffic types, multi-path forwarding optimizes resource utilization. Time-sensitive control messages and real-time telemetry utilize low-latency paths. Historical data synchronization and software updates leverage high-bandwidth paths. When multiple cellular carriers serve a location, SD-WAN distributes traffic across carriers, reducing dependence on any single provider.

Application-Aware Routing: SD-WAN solutions identify applications through deep packet inspection and route traffic based on application-specific policies. Voice and video conferencing applications receive priority and route over paths with appropriate latency and jitter characteristics. Critical IoT control protocols receive priority over less time-sensitive telemetry uploads. Bulk data transfers utilize best-effort paths, yielding capacity to higher-priority traffic.

Application identification in IoT contexts must recognize specialized protocols that standard DPI engines may not understand. Custom application definitions enable SD-WAN systems to properly classify and route IoT-specific protocols. Signature updates accommodate emerging protocols as IoT ecosystems evolve.

SD-WAN Security Features for IoT Gateways

Beyond connectivity optimization, SD-WAN platforms implement security capabilities that enhance IoT gateway protection and provide secure communication channels to cloud infrastructure.

Integrated Encryption and Tunnel Establishment: SD-WAN solutions establish encrypted overlay networks connecting distributed gateways to data centers and cloud platforms. IPsec or proprietary encryption protocols protect data in transit, preventing eavesdropping and tampering. Unlike traditional VPNs requiring manual tunnel configuration, SD-WAN platforms automatically establish and maintain encrypted tunnels based on network topology and policies.

Zero-touch tunnel establishment simplifies deployment of IoT gateways at scale. New gateways automatically discover controllers, authenticate using pre-provisioned certificates, and establish encrypted tunnels without manual configuration. This automation reduces deployment time and eliminates configuration errors that might compromise security.

Integrated Firewall and Security Services: Many SD-WAN platforms integrate firewall capabilities, providing security enforcement at gateway locations. Next-generation firewall features including application control, intrusion prevention, and URL filtering protect gateways from internet-based threats. Cloud-delivered security services augment on-premises capabilities with threat intelligence, malware analysis, and content filtering.

For IoT gateways, integrated security reduces complexity and cost compared to deploying separate security appliances. Unified management of networking and security functions through common platforms simplifies operations. Security policies follow workloads, with centralized definition and consistent enforcement across distributed locations.

Segmentation and Isolation: SD-WAN platforms support network segmentation through VPN overlays, creating isolated virtual networks over shared physical infrastructure. Different device classes, applications, or tenants can be assigned to separate segments with distinct security policies and access controls. Segmentation limits lateral movement and contains breaches within isolated segments.

In IoT contexts, segmentation separates device traffic from corporate networks, isolates different classes of IoT devices, and provides tenant isolation in multi-tenant deployments. Operational technology devices communicate over dedicated segments isolated from information technology networks. Guest or public-facing IoT devices operate in separate segments from internal devices.

Secure Local Breakout: Traditional hub-and-spoke WAN architectures backhaul all traffic to central data centers for security inspection before allowing internet access. This approach creates bandwidth bottlenecks and unnecessary latency for cloud-destined traffic. SD-WAN enables secure local internet breakout, where traffic destined for cloud services accesses the internet directly from gateway locations.

For IoT gateways communicating primarily with cloud platforms, local breakout dramatically reduces latency and improves user experience. Integrated security services at gateways inspect locally-broken-out traffic, maintaining security while eliminating backhauling overhead. Cloud-delivered security services provide inspection capabilities without requiring on-premises security infrastructure.

8.9 Quality of Service and Performance Optimization

IoT applications generate diverse traffic types with varying performance requirements. Industrial control systems require low latency and high reliability. Video surveillance generates high bandwidth demands. Sensor telemetry tolerates latency but requires reliable delivery. SD-WAN's quality of service and performance optimization capabilities ensure each traffic type receives appropriate treatment.

Dynamic Path Selection: SD-WAN platforms continuously monitor link characteristics including latency, jitter, packet loss, and available bandwidth. Traffic is dynamically routed over paths meeting application requirements. Real-time traffic experiencing degradation on the current path is moved to alternate paths with better characteristics. This dynamic path selection maximizes application performance despite varying link conditions.

For IoT deployments across diverse geographic locations with heterogeneous connectivity, dynamic path selection ensures consistent application experience. Locations with excellent connectivity leverage it for optimal performance. Locations with challenged connectivity adapt gracefully, utilizing available capacity effectively.

Forward Error Correction and Packet Duplication: Some SD-WAN solutions implement forward error correction (FEC) and packet duplication to improve reliability over lossy links. FEC transmits redundant data enabling reconstruction of lost packets without retransmission. Packet duplication sends critical traffic over multiple paths simultaneously, ensuring delivery despite individual path failures.

These techniques benefit IoT applications operating over unreliable connectivity like cellular or satellite links. Critical control messages or high-value telemetry can be protected through duplication, ensuring delivery despite intermittent connectivity issues. The overhead of FEC and duplication is selectively applied to traffic justifying the additional bandwidth consumption.

Traffic Shaping and Prioritization: SD-WAN platforms implement sophisticated traffic shaping and prioritization, allocating bandwidth according to business priorities. Critical traffic receives guaranteed bandwidth allocations. Lower-priority traffic utilizes remaining capacity but yields when congestion occurs. Rate limiting prevents individual applications or device classes from monopolizing bandwidth.

IoT environments with devices generating unpredictable traffic patterns benefit from traffic shaping. Surveillance cameras generating variable bitrate video don't starve critical control traffic. Bulk firmware update traffic is rate-limited to preserve capacity for operational traffic. Device classes generating excessive traffic due to misconfiguration or compromise are automatically throttled.

Centralized Management and Orchestration

Managing thousands of distributed IoT gateways through traditional device-by-device configuration would be operationally infeasible. SD-WAN's centralized management and orchestration capabilities provide the scalability required for large IoT deployments.

Zero-Touch Provisioning: SD-WAN platforms support zero-touch provisioning where gateways automatically configure themselves upon connection to networks. Gateways ship from manufacturers with bootstrap configurations enabling them to discover controllers. After discovery, gateways download operational configurations, establish secure tunnels, and begin forwarding traffic—all without technician intervention.

For IoT deployments across hundreds or thousands of locations, zero-touch provisioning dramatically reduces deployment time and cost. Gateways can be shipped directly to remote sites where non-technical personnel perform basic physical installation. The gateways self-configure, eliminating the need for skilled technicians at every location.

Template-Based Configuration: Rather than configuring each gateway individually, administrators define configuration templates that apply to groups of devices. Templates specify policies, routing behavior, security settings, and application treatment. New gateways automatically receive appropriate configurations based on their assignment to template groups. Configuration changes propagate automatically to all devices using affected templates.

Template-based management provides consistency across device fleets while enabling customization where needed. Standard templates ensure consistent security policies and operational behavior. Site-specific overrides accommodate unique local requirements without requiring fully custom configurations.

Centralized Visibility and Analytics: SD-WAN management platforms provide centralized visibility into network performance, application behavior, and security events across distributed gateways. Dashboards display aggregate metrics and detailed per-site information. Analytics identify performance issues, capacity constraints, and security threats. Automated alerting notifies operators of conditions requiring attention.

For IoT deployments, centralized visibility enables operational monitoring at scale. Bandwidth utilization trends inform capacity planning. Application performance metrics validate that IoT applications receive adequate service levels. Security dashboards highlight gateways experiencing attacks or unusual traffic patterns. Historical data supports troubleshooting and forensic analysis.

Automated Remediation and Self-Healing: Advanced SD-WAN platforms implement automated remediation capabilities that respond to detected issues without operator intervention. Link failures trigger automatic failover to backup paths. Performance degradation initiates dynamic rerouting. Security events trigger policy adjustments that mitigate threats. This self-healing behavior reduces mean time to repair and minimizes operational overhead.

IoT gateways in remote locations particularly benefit from self-healing capabilities. Locations lacking on-site technical staff continue operating despite equipment failures or network issues. Automated remediation handles routine issues, escalating only complex problems requiring operator attention. This automation dramatically improves operational efficiency for large-scale deployments.

Cloud Integration and Hybrid Connectivity

Modern IoT architectures increasingly leverage cloud platforms for device management, data storage, and analytics. SD-WAN facilitates cloud integration through optimized connectivity to major cloud providers and support for hybrid architectures spanning on-premises and cloud infrastructure.

Cloud On-Ramps and Optimized Cloud Access: SD-WAN platforms integrate with cloud providers through co-location facilities or direct interconnects, providing optimized paths to cloud platforms. Rather than accessing clouds over public internet, traffic utilizes private interconnects with lower latency, higher reliability, and enhanced security. Cloud on-ramps in multiple geographic regions enable location-aware routing to nearest cloud access points.

For cloud-centric IoT architectures, optimized cloud access significantly improves performance and reduces costs. Data uploads from gateways to cloud storage platforms complete faster and more reliably. API calls to cloud device management services experience lower latency. Egress fees may be reduced when using private interconnects rather than public internet paths.

Multi-Cloud Support: Many organizations adopt multi-cloud strategies, utilizing services from multiple providers or maintaining redundancy across clouds. SD-WAN platforms with multi-cloud support provide unified connectivity to AWS, Azure, Google Cloud, and other providers. Application-aware routing directs traffic to appropriate clouds based on application requirements and business policies.

IoT deployments leveraging multiple clouds benefit from SD-WAN's unified connectivity model. Device telemetry might flow to one cloud for storage while analytics workloads execute in another cloud. Control commands originate from yet another cloud platform. SD-WAN abstracts this complexity, presenting a consistent network regardless of underlying cloud topology.

Edge Computing Integration: Edge computing architectures deploy compute resources at or near IoT gateways, processing data locally rather than transmitting everything to cloud data centers. SD-WAN platforms support edge computing through integration with edge infrastructure, providing connectivity between edge compute nodes and facilitating data exchange with central systems when needed.

Hybrid architectures combining edge and cloud processing rely on SD-WAN to seamlessly span environments. Time-sensitive processing occurs at the edge with SD-WAN providing low-latency connectivity between edge devices and compute. Aggregate analytics and long-term storage occur in cloud with SD-WAN efficiently uploading relevant data. The SD-WAN layer enables applications to leverage edge and cloud resources as appropriate without requiring application-layer awareness of network topology.

Implementation Considerations for IoT Environments

Deploying SD-WAN for IoT gateway connectivity requires careful consideration of IoT-specific requirements and constraints that may differ from traditional enterprise SD-WAN deployments.

Gateway Integration Models: SD-WAN functionality can be integrated with IoT gateways through several models. Purpose-built IoT gateways may include integrated SD-WAN capabilities, combining protocol translation, edge processing, and WAN connectivity in unified devices. Alternatively, standalone SD-WAN appliances can be deployed alongside IoT gateways, providing WAN services to gateways via local connectivity. Virtual SD-WAN instances running on gateway compute platforms offer software-based integration.

The choice of integration model depends on gateway capabilities, scale requirements, and operational preferences. Integrated solutions reduce hardware footprint and simplify management. Standalone appliances provide flexibility to independently scale networking and IoT capabilities. Virtual instances maximize resource utilization but require gateway platforms with adequate compute capacity.

Power and Environmental Constraints: IoT gateways often deploy in challenging environments with limited power availability, extreme temperatures, or exposure to dust and moisture. SD-WAN solutions for IoT must accommodate these constraints through low-power operation, fanless designs, wide operating temperature ranges, and ruggedized enclosures suitable for industrial environments.

Power consumption particularly matters for remote locations powered by solar or battery systems. SD-WAN devices for such deployments should support power-saving modes, efficient operation under partial load, and graceful degradation when power availability is constrained. Environmental ratings appropriate for deployment conditions—IP-rated enclosures for outdoor deployment, conformal coating for corrosive environments—ensure reliable operation in diverse conditions.

Cellular and Alternative Connectivity: Unlike enterprise locations with fiber or cable connectivity, IoT gateways frequently rely on cellular networks as primary or backup connectivity. SD-WAN solutions must effectively utilize cellular links while managing associated challenges like data caps, variable latency, and limited bandwidth. Cellular-optimized features include aggressive header compression, intelligent traffic prioritization to maximize value of limited data, and monitoring of cellular signal strength and quality.

Alternative connectivity like satellite or fixed wireless may serve remote locations beyond cellular coverage. SD-WAN platforms should support diverse WAN interfaces and adapt behaviors to different link characteristics. High-latency satellite links require TCP optimization and protocol acceleration. Bandwidth-constrained fixed wireless benefits from aggressive compression and traffic shaping.

Scale and Economics: IoT deployments may span thousands to millions of gateways, dramatically exceeding scale of typical enterprise SD-WAN deployments. SD-WAN solutions for IoT must provide management platforms capable of operating at this scale while maintaining economic viability. Licensing models should align with IoT economics, avoiding per-device costs that become prohibitive at scale. Cloud-managed solutions amortize infrastructure costs across large deployments, improving economics compared to self-hosted management platforms.

Operational costs must also be considered. Cellular data consumption directly impacts ongoing costs; SD-WAN efficiency in utilizing cellular capacity affects total cost of ownership. Automation reduces operational costs associated with managing large device fleets. Open standards and multi-vendor support prevent vendor lock-in and enable cost optimization through competitive sourcing.

Chapter 9

Zero Trust and SASE Implementation With SD-WAN

9.1 Introduction

The convergence of networking and security has become imperative in today's distributed enterprise landscape. Traditional perimeter-based security models, designed for centralized data centers, have proven inadequate for environments where applications reside in multiple clouds, users work remotely, and branch offices require direct internet access. This chapter explores the integration of Zero Trust Network Access (ZTNA) and Secure Access Service Edge (SASE) frameworks with Software-Defined Wide Area Networks (SD-WAN), creating a comprehensive architecture that addresses modern connectivity and security challenges.

The Zero Trust philosophy—"never trust, always verify"—fundamentally changes how organizations approach network security. Rather than assuming trust based on network location, Zero Trust requires continuous verification of identity, device posture, and contextual factors before granting access to resources. When combined with SD-WAN's intelligent path selection and application-aware routing, and SASE's cloud-delivered security services, organizations can achieve unprecedented levels of security, performance, and agility.

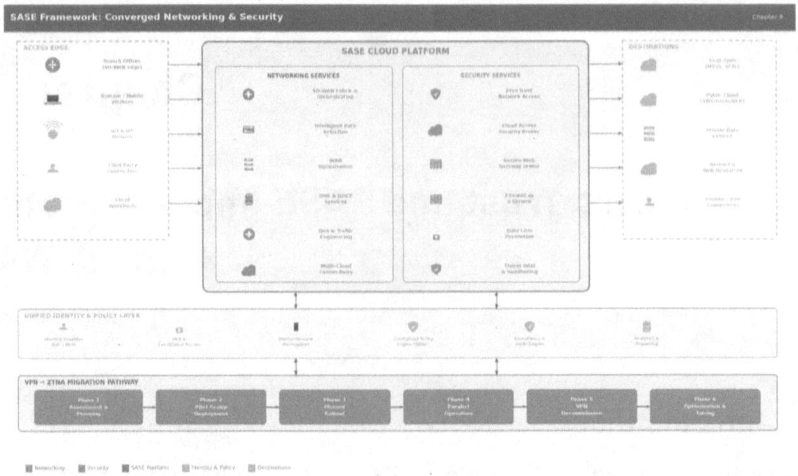

Figure 9.1: SASE Framework — Converged Networking, Security & Zero Trust

9.2 Architecting a SASE Framework: Convergence of Network and Security

Understanding SASE Architecture

Secure Access Service Edge (SASE) represents a paradigm shift in how organizations deliver network and security services. Coined by Gartner in 2019, SASE converges WAN capabilities with comprehensive security functions including Secure Web Gateway (SWG), Cloud Access Security Broker (CASB), Firewall as a Service (FWaaS), and Zero Trust Network Access into a unified cloud-native service model.

The SASE Architecture Consists of Several Foundational Components

Network Services Layer: This encompasses SD-WAN capabilities that provide intelligent routing, WAN optimization, bandwidth aggregation, and quality of service management. SD-WAN forms the underlying transport mechanism, enabling dynamic path selection based on application requirements and network conditions.

Security Services Layer: Cloud-delivered security functions operate at the edge, inspecting traffic close to users and applications. These services include next-generation firewalls, intrusion prevention systems, data loss prevention, malware protection, and SSL/TLS inspection. By delivering security from the cloud, organizations eliminate the need for backhauling traffic to centralized data centers.

Identity and Policy Engine: At the heart of SASE lies a robust identity management system that enforces granular access policies. This engine integrates with enterprise identity providers, evaluates contextual factors, and makes real-time access decisions based on comprehensive risk assessment.

Management and Orchestration Plane: A unified management console provides visibility across the entire SASE fabric, enabling policy configuration, monitoring, analytics, and incident response from a single pane of glass.

Core Principles of SASE Convergence

The convergence of networking and security in SASE is guided by several fundamental principles:

Identity-Centric Architecture: Traditional network security focused on IP addresses and network segments. SASE shifts this paradigm to identity as the primary control plane. Users, devices, and applications possess verified identities, and policies are enforced based on these identities rather than network location.

Cloud-Native Delivery: SASE services are delivered from globally distributed points of presence (PoPs), ensuring low latency and high availability. This cloud-native approach enables elastic scaling, rapid deployment of new capabilities, and consistent policy enforcement regardless of where users or applications reside.

Context-Aware Policy Enforcement: Access decisions consider multiple contextual factors beyond simple authentication. Device posture, location, time of access, application sensitivity, and real-time threat intelligence all inform policy decisions, creating adaptive security that responds to changing risk profiles.

Data-Centric Security: Protection follows the data rather than relying on network perimeter defenses. Whether data resides in SaaS applications, IaaS environments, or on-premises systems, consistent security policies apply, preventing unauthorized access and data exfiltration.

Implementing SASE with SD-WAN Integration

Integrating SD-WAN with SASE requires careful architectural planning. Organizations must consider several implementation models:

Edge-Based SASE: In this model, SD-WAN appliances at branch locations incorporate security functions locally while leveraging cloud-based services for advanced threat protection and policy management. This approach minimizes latency for local traffic while maintaining centralized control.

Cloud-First SASE: Traffic is directed from SD-WAN edges to nearby SASE PoPs where comprehensive security inspection occurs. This model simplifies branch infrastructure, reduces hardware footprint, and ensures consistent security regardless of traffic patterns.

Hybrid SASE: Organizations implement a combination of local and cloud-based security, optimizing for performance and compliance requirements. Critical or latency-sensitive traffic may undergo local inspection, while other traffic is directed to cloud security services.

The Integration Architecture Typically Involves

1. SD-WAN Fabric Establishment: Deploy SD-WAN infrastructure across branch offices, data centers, and cloud environments, creating an overlay network with intelligent routing capabilities.

2. SASE PoP Integration: Configure SD-WAN tunnels to SASE provider PoPs, establishing secure connections for traffic forwarding and policy enforcement.
3. Policy Orchestration: Define unified policies that span networking and security functions, ensuring consistent enforcement across the SASE fabric.
4. Identity Integration: Connect SASE architecture with enterprise identity systems (Active Directory, Azure AD, Okta, etc.) to enable identity-based access control.
5. Application Discovery and Classification: Implement deep packet inspection and application recognition to identify traffic flows and apply appropriate policies.

Design Considerations and Best Practices

Successful SASE implementation requires attention to several design considerations:

PoP Proximity and Coverage: Select SASE providers with PoPs geographically close to users and critical applications. Latency introduced by routing traffic to distant PoPs can negate the performance benefits of SD-WAN.

Bandwidth and Scalability: Ensure SASE infrastructure can handle peak traffic loads without bottlenecks. Cloud-based security services must scale elastically to accommodate traffic growth.

Inspection Depth vs. Performance: Balance comprehensive security inspection with performance requirements. SSL/TLS decryption and deep packet inspection consume significant resources; organizations must determine appropriate inspection policies for different traffic types.

Failure Modes and Redundancy: Design for high availability with redundant SASE PoPs and failover mechanisms. SD-WAN should maintain connectivity even if primary SASE services become unavailable.

Regulatory Compliance: Consider data residency and sovereignty requirements. Some industries or regions mandate that data remain within specific geographic boundaries, influencing SASE PoP selection and traffic routing.

9.3 Implementing ZTNA on the SD-WAN Fabric

Zero Trust Network Access Fundamentals

Zero Trust Network Access redefines how users and devices access applications and resources. Unlike VPNs that grant broad network access upon successful authentication, ZTNA implements micro segmentation and least-privilege access, connecting specific users to specific applications based on granular policies.

ZTNA Operates on Several Core Principles

Explicit Verification: Every access request undergoes authentication and authorization, regardless of the requestor's location. Trust is never implicit based on network position.

Least Privilege Access: Users receive minimal access necessary to perform their functions. Rather than connecting to entire network segments, users establish direct, encrypted connections to authorized applications only.

Assumed Breach Mentality: The architecture assumes that threats exist both outside and inside the network perimeter. Continuous monitoring and verification prevent lateral movement and contain potential breaches.

ZTNA Architecture on SD-WAN

Implementing ZTNA on an SD-WAN fabric involves several architectural components:

ZTNA Controllers: Centralized controllers manage policies, authenticate users and devices, and broker connections between requestors and resources. These controllers integrate with identity providers and policy engines to make access decisions.

SD-WAN Edge as Enforcement Point: SD-WAN appliances at branch locations act as policy enforcement points, applying ZTNA policies to user traffic. When users attempt to access applications, SD-WAN edges consult ZTNA controllers for authorization decisions.

Application Connectors: Lightweight agents deployed near protected applications establish outbound connections to ZTNA controllers. These connectors receive inbound user connections and forward authorized traffic to applications, eliminating the need for inbound firewall rules.

Identity Providers Integration: ZTNA solutions integrate with enterprise identity systems, enabling Single Sign-On (SSO) and Multi-Factor Authentication (MFA). Authentication tokens validate user identities throughout the access session.

Context-Aware Access Policies

ZTNA policies extend beyond simple user authentication to incorporate rich contextual information:

User Context: Policies consider user roles, group memberships, and attributes from identity systems. Access permissions adapt based on organizational hierarchy, department affiliation, or specific job functions.

Device Context: Device posture assessment evaluates compliance with security standards before granting access. Policies verify operating system versions, installed security software, encryption status, and the presence of known vulnerabilities. Non-compliant devices receive restricted or denied access.

Application Context: Access policies vary based on application sensitivity. Critical applications may require higher authentication assurance levels, specific device compliance standards, or geographic restrictions.

Behavioral Context: Advanced ZTNA implementations leverage user and entity behavior analytics (UEBA) to detect anomalous access patterns. Unusual login times, locations, or data access patterns trigger additional verification or access restrictions.

Risk Score Integration: Many ZTNA solutions calculate real-time risk scores based on multiple factors. High-risk scores may trigger step-up authentication, restrict access, or alert security teams for investigation.

Policy Configuration Examples

Implementing effective ZTNA policies requires careful planning and configuration. Consider these examples:

Financial Application Access Policy

- User: Finance department members
- Device: Corporate-managed devices with full-disk encryption, updated antivirus, and compliant OS
- MFA: Required for all access attempts
- Location: Restricted to approved countries
- Time: Business hours only, with exceptions for approved users
- Action: Grant access to financial ERP application only; deny access to underlying network

Partner Access Policy

- User: External contractors or partners
- Device: Personal devices meeting minimum security baseline
- MFA: Required with SMS or authenticator app
- Location: Any
- Time: Contract validity period only
- Action: Grant access to collaboration tools and specific project resources; deny access to internal systems

Administrative Access Policy

- User: IT administrators
- Device: Privileged Access Workstations (PAWs) with hardened configurations
- MFA: Required with hardware tokens
- Location: From corporate offices or approved VPN
- Time: Any, with logging of all access
- Action: Grant access to management interfaces; require re-authentication for sensitive operations

Microsegmentation with SD-WAN and ZTNA

Microsegmentation divides networks into small, isolated zones, limiting lateral movement in case of compromise. Implementing microsegmentation on SD-WAN with ZTNA involves:

Application-Centric Segments: Rather than traditional VLAN-based segmentation, create application-centric segments where access is controlled by ZTNA policies. Each application becomes a distinct segment accessible only through authorized ZTNA connections.

Dynamic Segmentation: Leverage SD-WAN's programmability to create and modify segments dynamically based on changing business requirements. New applications automatically receive appropriate segmentation policies.

East-West Traffic Control: While ZTNA primarily addresses remote access (north-south traffic), microsegmentation also controls traffic between internal resources (east-west). SD-WAN enforces policies for inter-application communication, preventing unauthorized lateral movement.

Monitoring and Analytics

Effective ZTNA implementation requires comprehensive monitoring:

Access Logs: Maintain detailed logs of all access requests, including granted and denied attempts. These logs support forensic analysis and compliance reporting.

Anomaly Detection: Implement behavioral analytics to identify unusual access patterns. Machine learning algorithms establish baselines and flag deviations for investigation.

Performance Metrics: Monitor connection establishment times, application response times, and user experience metrics to ensure ZTNA doesn't negatively impact productivity.

Policy Effectiveness: Regularly review policy configurations and access patterns to identify overly permissive or restrictive policies requiring adjustment.

9.4 Identity and Access Management (IAM) Integration

The Role of IAM in ZTNA/SASE

Identity and Access Management forms the foundation of Zero Trust architectures. IAM systems provide the authoritative source of user identities, attributes, and entitlements that drive access decisions across the SASE fabric. Seamless integration between IAM and networking infrastructure enables consistent policy enforcement regardless of how users connect or where resources reside.

IAM Components and Architecture

A comprehensive IAM architecture for ZTNA/SASE integration includes:

Identity Providers (IdP): Centralized identity repositories such as Active Directory, Azure Active Directory, Okta, or Ping Identity store user credentials, attributes, and group memberships. These systems authenticate users and provide identity assertions to downstream applications and services.

Multi-Factor Authentication (MFA): MFA systems add authentication factors beyond passwords, requiring possession (hardware tokens, mobile devices), biometrics (fingerprint, facial recognition), or location verification. MFA significantly reduces credential compromise risks.

Single Sign-On (SSO): SSO solutions enable users to authenticate once and access multiple applications without repeated login prompts. SAML, OAuth, and OpenID Connect protocols facilitate identity federation across cloud and on-premises applications.

Privileged Access Management (PAM): PAM systems control administrative access to critical systems, implementing additional security controls such as session recording, just-in-time access provisioning, and credential vaulting.

Directory Services: LDAP-based directories store organizational hierarchies, group memberships, and user attributes that inform access decisions. Modern implementations may include cloud directories that federate with on-premises systems.

Integration Patterns

Integrating IAM with ZTNA and SD-WAN involves several technical patterns:

SAML-Based Federation: Security Assertion Markup Language (SAML) enables identity federation between IAM systems and ZTNA controllers. When users attempt to access applications through ZTNA, controllers redirect them to the enterprise IdP for authentication. Upon successful authentication, the IdP issues a SAML assertion containing user attributes and group memberships. The ZTNA controller validates this assertion and makes access decisions based on configured policies.

RADIUS Integration: For network access control at SD-WAN edges, Remote Authentication Dial-In User Service (RADIUS) provides authentication services. SD-WAN appliances act as RADIUS clients, forwarding authentication requests to RADIUS servers that validate credentials against enterprise directories. This pattern supports legacy applications and network devices that lack modern authentication protocol support.

OAuth and OpenID Connect: Modern cloud applications leverage OAuth 2.0 for authorization and OpenID Connect for authentication. ZTNA solutions implement these protocols to obtain access tokens from IAM systems, enabling fine-grained access control without directly handling user credentials.

Directory Synchronization: For organizations with multiple identity sources, directory synchronization tools maintain consistency across systems. Azure AD Connect, for example, synchronizes on-premises Active Directory with Azure AD, enabling hybrid cloud identity management.

Policy Synchronization and Enforcement

Effective IAM integration requires synchronizing policies across IAM and networking systems:

Attribute-Based Access Control (ABAC): Rather than simply checking group memberships, ABAC policies evaluate multiple users, resource, and environmental attributes. For example, a policy might grant access only if the user is a manager (role attribute), accessing from a corporate device (device attribute), during business hours (time attribute), and connecting from an approved location (location attribute).

Role-Based Access Control (RBAC): Traditional RBAC assigns permissions based on organizational roles. IAM systems define roles and associated entitlements, while ZTNA controllers enforce these roles across network and application access.

Policy Decision Points: Centralized policy decision points evaluate access requests against configured rules. These components query IAM systems for user attributes, device compliance systems for posture information, and threat intelligence for risk data, combining these inputs to make authorization decisions.

Policy Enforcement Points: SD-WAN edges and ZTNA gateways act as policy enforcement points, implementing decisions from policy decision points. This separation ensures consistent policy logic while enabling distributed enforcement close to users and applications.

Just-In-Time (JIT) Access and Privilege Elevation

Modern IAM systems support dynamic privilege elevation for administrative access:

Request and Approval Workflows: Users request elevated privileges through self-service portals. Approval workflows route requests to appropriate managers or security teams for review. Upon approval, temporary elevated permissions are provisioned.

Time-Bound Access: Elevated privileges expire automatically after a configured period, implementing the principle of least privilege. Users must request extensions if additional time is needed.

Breakglass Access: Emergency access procedures enable privileged access during critical incidents when normal approval workflows would cause unacceptable delays. All breakglass access undergoes intensive logging and post-incident review.

Continuous Authentication and Adaptive Access

Zero Trust extends beyond initial authentication to continuous verification:

Session Monitoring: Rather than granting unlimited access after initial authentication, continuous authentication monitors ongoing sessions for anomalies. Unusual behavior triggers re-authentication or access termination.

Risk-Based Authentication: Adaptive authentication systems calculate real-time risk scores based on context. Low-risk access (familiar device, typical location, normal hours) may require only password authentication. High-risk scenarios (new device, unusual location, sensitive data access) trigger step-up authentication with additional factors.

Conditional Access Policies: IAM systems implement conditional access rules that modify authentication requirements based on context. For example, users accessing applications from corporate networks may require only SSO, while remote access mandates MFA.

Identity Governance and Compliance

IAM integration supports governance and compliance requirements:

Access Certification: Regular access reviews ensure users maintain only appropriate entitlements. Managers periodically review and certify access for their team members, identifying and removing excessive permissions.

Segregation of Duties (SoD): Policies prevent conflicting privileges that could enable fraud. For example, users cannot both initiate and approve financial transactions.

Audit Logging: Comprehensive logs capture all authentication attempts, authorization decisions, and access activities. These logs support compliance reporting for regulations such as SOX, HIPAA, and GDPR.

Lifecycle Management: Automated provisioning and deprovisioning ensure timely access grants and revocations. When employees join, transfer, or leave the organization, IAM systems automatically adjust network access entitlements.

9.5 Edge Computing and Security at the SD-WAN Branch

Edge Computing in SD-WAN Architecture

Edge computing brings computational resources and services closer to users and data sources, reducing latency and bandwidth consumption while improving application performance. In SD-WAN environments, branch office edges represent strategic locations for deploying security and application services.

Security Functions at the Edge

Implementing security functions directly at SD-WAN branch edges provides several advantages:

Local Internet Breakout Security: Traditional hub-and-spoke architectures backhaul internet traffic to data centers for security inspection, introducing latency and consuming WAN bandwidth. Edge security enables direct internet access from branches with local firewall, intrusion prevention, and content filtering, improving cloud application performance while maintaining security.

SSL/TLS Inspection: Encrypted traffic inspection at the edge ensures visibility into HTTPS sessions without the bandwidth overhead of backhauling encrypted traffic to centralized security infrastructure. Modern SD-WAN appliances incorporate SSL inspection capabilities, decrypting traffic, inspecting for threats, and re-encrypting for transmission.

Advanced Threat Protection: Deploy sandboxing, anti-malware, and intrusion prevention systems at branch edges to detect and block sophisticated threats before they infiltrate the organization. Local threat prevention reduces exposure windows and limits the need for central security infrastructure scaling.

DNS Security: DNS-layer security at branches blocks malicious domains, prevents DNS tunneling, and provides visibility into DNS queries. This first line of defense stops many threats before users can access malicious sites.

Web Content Filtering: Enforce acceptable use policies locally, preventing access to inappropriate categories without requiring policy enforcement at distant locations. Categories include malware sites, phishing pages, adult content, and unauthorized cloud applications.

Edge Computing Use Cases

Beyond security, edge computing at SD-WAN branches supports various applications:

Application Performance Optimization: Deploy WAN optimization techniques locally, including data deduplication, compression, protocol acceleration, and caching. These optimizations reduce bandwidth requirements and improve application responsiveness.

Local Data Processing: Process branch-generated data locally rather than transmitting raw data to centralized locations. Examples include retail point-of-sale analytics, manufacturing sensor data aggregation, and video surveillance storage.

IoT Gateway Functions: Branch edges serve as IoT gateways, aggregating data from sensors, industrial control systems, and connected devices. Local processing filters and preprocesses IoT data before selective transmission to cloud analytics platforms.

SD-WAN-as-a-Service Extensions: Cloud-managed SD-WAN enables rapid deployment of new services to branch edges through centralized orchestration. Organizations can deploy new security capabilities, application services, or compliance tools without on-site intervention.

Infrastructure Considerations

Implementing edge computing and security requires appropriate infrastructure:

Hardware Platforms: Select SD-WAN appliances with sufficient CPU, memory, and storage for planned edge services. Some security functions, particularly SSL inspection and sandboxing, demand substantial computational resources. Hardware selection must account for peak loads with headroom for growth.

Virtualization Support: Many modern SD-WAN platforms support virtual network functions (VNFs), enabling deployment of third-party security and application services on the same hardware. This consolidation reduces branch infrastructure footprint and simplifies management.

High Availability: Implement redundant SD-WAN appliances at critical branches to ensure continuous security and connectivity. Active-active or active-passive configurations maintain services during hardware failures.

Power and Cooling: Edge computing increases power consumption and heat generation at branches. Ensure adequate electrical capacity and cooling in branch equipment rooms.

Balancing Local vs. Cloud Security

Organizations must determine the optimal distribution of security functions between branch edges and cloud services:

Latency-Sensitive Decisions: Local security enforcement minimizes latency for time-sensitive operations. Initial threat blocking, URL filtering, and basic firewall functions benefit from edge implementation.

Resource-Intensive Analysis: Cloud-delivered security services provide the computational scale for advanced threat analysis, sandboxing, and machine learning-based detection. These services analyze threats across the entire customer base, enabling faster threat response.

Hybrid Approaches: Many implementations combine edge and cloud security. Basic filtering and known-threat blocking occur locally, while suspicious content is forwarded to cloud services for deep analysis. This hybrid model balances performance and security depth.

Managing Edge Security at Scale

Centralized management is essential when security functions are distributed to numerous branch locations:

Zero-Touch Provisioning: New branch appliances self-configure upon installation, downloading configurations and security policies from cloud management platforms. This approach eliminates manual configuration and reduces deployment time from weeks to hours.

Policy Synchronization: Centralized policy management ensures consistent security enforcement across all branches. Policy changes propagate automatically, maintaining uniform protection without manual updates to each location.

Software Updates: Automated update mechanisms ensure edge appliances receive timely security patches and feature updates. Staged rollouts test updates on pilot sites before broader deployment, minimizing disruption risks.

Monitoring and Alerting: Centralized security operations centers (SOCs) monitor events from all branch edges, correlating alerts and identifying threats that span multiple locations. Security information and event management (SIEM) systems aggregate logs for comprehensive visibility.

Regulatory and Compliance Considerations

Edge security implementation must address compliance requirements:

Data Residency: Some regulations mandate that data remain within specific geographic boundaries. Organizations must ensure that edge security processes data locally when required, avoiding transmission to cloud services in other jurisdictions.

Audit Trails: Maintain comprehensive logs of security events, policy changes, and administrative actions at branch edges. These logs support compliance audits and forensic investigations.

Encryption Standards: Implement appropriate encryption for data in transit and at rest. Ensure that edge security functions, particularly SSL inspection, comply with organizational and regulatory encryption policies.

9.6 Practical Steps for Migrating from Traditional VPN to ZTNA/SD-WAN

Migration Planning and Assessment

Transitioning from traditional VPN architectures to ZTNA with SD-WAN represents a significant undertaking that requires methodical planning:

Current State Assessment: Begin by documenting the existing VPN infrastructure, including concentrators, authentication systems, user populations, applications accessed through VPNs, and bandwidth utilization patterns. Understanding the current environment identifies migration requirements and potential challenges.

Application Inventory: Catalog all applications users access remotely. Classify applications by protocol (web, client-server, legacy), authentication method, sensitivity level, and user population. This inventory drives ZTNA policy design and migration prioritization.

User Segmentation: Identify distinct user populations with different access requirements. Typical segments include employees, contractors, partners, and administrators. Each segment may require different migration approaches and timelines.

Network Dependencies: Document application dependencies, including database connections, file shares, and inter-application communications. ZTNA's application-centric approach requires understanding these dependencies to ensure connectivity post-migration.

Compliance Requirements: Review regulatory and compliance obligations affecting remote access. Some industries face specific requirements for authentication strength, data encryption, or audit logging that influence ZTNA design.

Migration Strategy Selection

Organizations can adopt different migration approaches based on their circumstances:

Phased Migration by User Group: Migrate users in waves, starting with pilot groups and progressively expanding to larger populations. This approach minimizes disruption and allows learning from early phases to improve subsequent deployments. Begin with technical users who can provide detailed feedback, then expand to other departments.

Phased Migration by Application: Migrate applications individually or in groups, running VPN and ZTNA concurrently during the transition. Users may access some applications through ZTNA while continuing to use VPNs for others. This approach works well when applications have distinct user populations or migration complexity varies significantly.

Parallel Operation: Maintain both VPN and ZTNA indefinitely, allowing users to choose their access method. While this approach provides maximum flexibility and minimal disruption, it increases operational complexity and may delay full ZTNA benefit realization.

Direct Cutover: Replace VPN with ZTNA in a single transition. This approach suits smaller deployments or organizations with high change tolerance. Careful planning and extensive testing are essential to minimize disruption.

Infrastructure Preparation

Before migrating users, prepare the necessary infrastructure:

ZTNA Controller Deployment: Deploy ZTNA controllers in highly available configurations. Cloud-based ZTNA services simplify deployment, while on-premises controllers provide greater control for organizations with specific requirements.

SD-WAN Fabric Establishment: If not already deployed, implement SD-WAN across branch offices, data centers, and cloud environments. Ensure adequate bandwidth and configure application-aware routing policies.

Application Connector Installation: Deploy application connectors for each application that users will access through ZTNA. Connectors typically install near applications, either on dedicated servers or as virtual machines. For SaaS applications, configure ZTNA provider integrations.

Identity System Integration: Connect ZTNA controllers to enterprise identity providers. Configure SAML or OIDC federation, test authentication flows, and establish attribute mappings that will drive access policies.

Certificate Infrastructure: Ensure proper SSL/TLS certificates are in place for ZTNA components. Users should not encounter certificate warnings that might train them to ignore security alerts.

Policy Design and Configuration

Develop comprehensive access policies that replace VPN's broad network access:

Start with Least Privilege: Begin with restrictive policies that grant access only to specific applications. Users should connect directly to applications rather than entire network segments. This approach minimizes the attack surface and prepares for future micro segmentation.

Map VPN Groups to ZTNA Policies: Existing VPN group policies provide a starting point for ZTNA policy design. However, avoid simply replicating VPN policies. ZTNA enables more granular control; leverage this capability to implement true least-privilege access.

Incorporate Device Posture: Define device compliance requirements for different application sensitivity levels. Critical applications should require corporate-managed devices with full-disk encryption and updated security software, while less sensitive applications might permit personal devices meeting basic security standards.

Configure MFA Requirements: Determine appropriate MFA requirements for different access scenarios. High-security applications or access from untrusted networks should mandate MFA, while access from corporate networks might leverage SSO.

Establish Monitoring and Alerting: Configure logging and alerting to detect policy violations, authentication failures, and anomalous access patterns. These controls provide visibility into the ZTNA environment and support incident response.

Pilot Deployment

Execute a controlled pilot before broader migration:

Pilot User Selection: Choose technically proficient pilot users who can provide detailed feedback. Include representatives from different departments to validate diverse application access requirements.

Communication and Training: Clearly communicate migration plans to pilot users. Provide training on the new access method, emphasizing any workflow changes. Establish feedback channels for users to report issues.

Monitoring and Issue Resolution: Closely monitor pilot deployment, tracking authentication success rates, application performance, and user feedback. Quickly address identified issues before expanding the migration.

Performance Validation: Verify that application performance meets or exceeds VPN-based access. ZTNA should improve performance for cloud applications by eliminating VPN backhaul, but some on-premises applications might require optimization.

Policy Refinement: Adjust policies based on pilot experience. Initial policies may prove too restrictive or too permissive; refine them before broader deployment.

Broad Migration Execution

After successful pilot validation, proceed with broader migration:

Communication Plan: Develop comprehensive communication to all users explaining the migration timeline, process, and benefits. Address common concerns about security, access changes, and support availability.

Phased Rollout: Migrate users or applications in planned waves. Monitor each phase before proceeding to ensure stability and address emerging issues.

Parallel Operation Period: Maintain VPN availability during initial ZTNA rollout, providing a fallback option if users encounter problems. This parallel operation reduces pressure and allows gradual transition.

User Support: Enhance support team training on ZTNA technology and common issues. Ensure adequate staffing during migration phases to handle increased support requests.

Documentation Updates: Update user documentation, IT procedures, and troubleshooting guides to reflect the new ZTNA environment.

VPN Decommissioning

Once ZTNA proves stable and users are successfully transitioned:

Usage Monitoring: Track VPN usage to identify users or applications not yet migrated. Investigate remaining VPN use cases to determine whether they represent migration gaps or legitimate exceptions.

Cutover Planning: Set a firm VPN decommissioning date, providing advance notice to users. This deadline motivates completion of remaining migrations and allows planning for any final edge cases.

Exception Handling: Some legacy systems or specific use cases might require continued VPN access. Document these exceptions, implement appropriate controls, and plan for eventual elimination.

Infrastructure Removal: Decommission VPN concentrators, update firewall rules to remove VPN-related configurations, and terminate VPN-related contracts or licenses. Ensure no security gaps emerge from infrastructure removal.

Post-Migration Optimization

After successful migration, focus on optimization and continuous improvement:

Policy Tuning: Regularly review access logs and policy effectiveness. Adjust policies to eliminate overly permissive rules while ensuring legitimate access remains efficient.

Performance Monitoring: Continuously monitor application performance and user experience. Address performance degradations promptly to maintain user satisfaction.

Security Enhancement: Leverage ZTNA's rich telemetry to implement advanced security controls. Deploy behavioral analytics, anomaly detection, and adaptive authentication policies that would be difficult in traditional VPN environments.

Compliance Reporting: Utilize ZTNA's detailed logging to streamline compliance reporting. Demonstrate least-privilege access, complete audit trails, and comprehensive authentication controls to auditors.

www.ingramcontent.com/pod-product-compliance
Lightning Source LLC
LaVergne TN
LVHW090322210926
848480LV00001B/330